The Dionne Quintuplets' Story

FROM BIRTH THROUGH GIRLHOOD
TO WOMANHOOD

"WE WERE FIVE"

BY

JAMES BROUGH

WITH

Annette, Cécile, Marie, and Yvonne Dionne

SIMON AND SCHUSTER
NEW YORK

PUBLISHED BY SIMON AND SCHUSTER, INC.
ROCKEFELLER CENTER, 630 FIFTH AVENUE
NEW YORK 20, N.Y.

MANUFACTURED IN THE UNITED STATES OF AMERICA

DESIGNED BY EDITH FOWLER

. . . And lead us not into temptation,
But deliver us from evil . . .

Illustration Section
follows page 64

❧ ONE ❧

I T IS EASY now for a stranger to visit Corbeil and not
know that we ever existed. Unless he arrives forewarned
and is curious enough to ask questions, it is unlikely that
our name will be mentioned to him by anyone. There is
no sign, no plaque, nothing at all in the village to mark
the fact that we passed this way once upon a time. Perhaps it is best that it ended like this.

The gray asphalt parking areas still sprawl beside the
road, but they are forever deserted. Every summer the
weeds creep in closer and reclaim a little more. The
paved highway they built to bring the world to our door
is humpbacked in places and cracked with the frosts of a
dozen and more years of neglect. It carries only a trickle
of farmers' trucks and an occasional tourist's car.

On the earth a few stubborn scars remain to tell where
the souvenir shacks once stood, and the intimidating,
steel-mesh fences, and the red log building shaped like
the letter U, where crowds waited in their thousands to
watch five little girls at play. After the years of tumult,

7

peace has long since returned to the village and to most of the people who live there.

To reach Corbeil, a visitor follows Route 11 north out of Toronto or Route 17 going northwest from Ottawa. One can drive quickly along those roads that pierce the undulating Laurentian landscape, through the wilderness of spruce and maple and pine, past the patchwork of rivers and lakes and little rock-bound farms, making perhaps for the white beaches and blue water of Lake Nipissing, which reaches its long arms up toward the Arctic Circle.

Fishermen head this way for speckled trout, pickerel, bass and muskellunge. In the fall, the hunters come for partridge and deer, and fog like cotton candy swirls in off the lake to blot out the sky at a minute's notice. There are bear and moose in these woods. In the winter, one can sometimes hear wolves.

In the old days, a fresh car would roll in off the highway every sixty seconds, from early morning until long after darkness, to climb the hill that leads to Corbeil. Twice a day, the flow of traffic thickened—just before we made our advertised appearances in the playground that lay at the heart of the U-shaped observation building, splashing in the paddling pool, pedaling our tricycles, scrambling up and over the bars of the jungle gym.

There is a story that Dad taught arithmetic to Oliva junior, who was born twenty-six months after us, by having him count the cars as they passed the front door of the little farmhouse with its red-shingle roof and ocher-stained walls, that stood across the road from the observatory. But that may be a legend like so much else.

Now the old house has gone, too. Another brother, Daniel, kept it open as a museum for a season or two, with some relics of our nursery days on view. Then he sold it, to be hauled away as some kind of souvenir of the past and, if anyone should be interested, opened to

8

sightseers willing to pay the price of admission. Mom would not have our baby things made part of the bargain. They were taken out before the moving men arrived.

On the grounds of a motel miles away, whose roadside sign promises "char-broiled steaks—single $6.50, double $9.00," the house stands now as an exceedingly weather-beaten tourist attraction, at the end of a sandy path. A painted board carried an invitation to "Visit the Birthplace of the Dionne Quints," but the wind blew it over. The porch sags forlornly, and its outside planks are all but bare of color. Between September and June, the place is padlocked. In the summer it is possible to go in, but the stranger might do better to patronize the trim miniature golf course on one side of the place or pay a quarter for a pony ride on the other.

Once inside the little frame house—fifty cents for adults and a dime for children—the stranger might still wonder if his money had been well spent. It is hard to imagine that anyone could have lived and died in these abandoned rooms. There on the left, he can walk through the doorless archway and inspect the spot on the creaking floorboards where the great bed stood. In the kitchen there is the big hooded stove and the cast-iron washing machine, handed down from an earlier generation, in which Mom pounded, who knows how many thousand times, the soiled clothes of her family. There is little else to catch the eye.

The parking lots on the Corbeil road used to be covered with cars, row after row of them. The license plates represented every province of Canada and every state in the Union. If gas was needed, it could be bought from a service station in Callander, the town a few miles down the road, where five pumps were lined up by the curb, labeled "Emilie," "Annette," "Marie," "Cécile" and

9

"Yvonne." It seems that we were an attraction comparable with Radio City or the Empire State Building.

They say that a hundred thousand people used to turn up every month in those past summers to see us. So long as they had made reservations early enough, they could put up at the new Red Line Inn or at the old Callander Hotel, which built on an extra story to take care of the throng. Thousands of people slept in tourist camps and cabins with names like "Baby View Pavilion," which sprang up for miles around. Over a holiday weekend from May through September, it was difficult to find a comfortable bed for the night much closer than a hundred miles away.

The smell of greed must have hung in the air like the odor of the hot dogs and popcorn that the peddlers sold to the sightseers. We dwelt at the center of a circus, a carnival set in the middle of nowhere. Clapboard shops and shanties of every size and shape sprouted as fast as mushrooms along the highway, to lure the crowds who, rain or shine, came to inspect us. Dad conducted the most ambitious of the stores, built on his own land directly across the road from the group of buildings that made up our home. He had twenty-five people on his payroll at one time. His souvenir store lost its roof in a winter gale and had to be demolished. We could see it from our windows. We were sad when it was gone; it was one of the familiar sights of our lives.

Those who wanted souvenirs—and who didn't?— could buy Scottish woolens, English bone china, Indian blankets, French knitted garments and every conceivable memento of the Quintuplets. There were spoons, cups, plates, plaques, candy bars, books, postcards, dolls and a hundred other items, most of them adorned, if the word is appropriate, with pictures of five children who looked like nobody we ever knew. It was Coney Island, a

10

World's Fair and Madison Square Garden rolled into one, so we gather, and we were the sole exhibit.

It was possible to examine "The Original Basket in Which the Dionne Babies Were Placed"—in the words of a crudely lettered card—or to rent binoculars, the better to see with. Someone once counted no less than three "original baskets" on display in various locations. One might pay fifty cents—and this was a thriving business in which Dad joined—for a stone that supposedly came from the Dionne farm and therefore, in the minds of the superstitious, must have acquired some magical power of fertility.

Of all the strange fancies that quintuplets stir in the minds of men, the regard for them as evidence of fertility is probably the strangest. Perhaps such feelings date back long, long ago, to the dark ages of savagery before Christianity arose in the world. In Corbeil there was no shortage of customers for fertility stones, which in truth were picked up from any field or roadside for sale to the ignorant and unsuspecting.

Dad and a number of family relatives and friends were also pleased to sell autographs and framed photographs for fifty cents and more apiece. A visitor, if he cared, could hear a dramatic account of what happened on May 28, 1934, direct from the lips of Aunt Donalda Legros, who was one of the two midwives attending Mom before the doctor arrived. Aunt Donalda needed little prompting to talk about it.

At first, only one wire fence surrounded us. Then it was decided by the distant beings who controlled our destinies that for safety's sake there should be two. For forty-five minutes each morning and afternoon, the gates in those two fences were unlocked, not to let us go out but to let the world come in. The uniformed guards who opened the gates ran the risk of being bowled over in the rush to get inside.

11

The visitors used to wait in the warm summer sun six abreast, thousands at a time, in a line that stretched as far as half a mile down the road. They waited impatiently, as if for a football game. They would stand by the hour for a few minutes' glimpse of us through the one-way screens that overlooked the playground from the interior of the long corridor that wound through the observation building. Those one-way screens were, in truth, two-way screens. We could always see through them, as one can see through frosted glass. We were always conscious of being watched, but we did not mind it in the least. Anyone wearing white showed up best. One or more of us would usually consider it polite to wave to the crowd. Emilie was a great one for waving.

When the gates swung open, the children who had been waiting usually raced ahead, to be first up the steps into the darkened observation corridors. Close after them came the young couples, then the middle-aged, followed by the very elderly, who somehow felt a special pull toward Corbeil, possibly because they were reminded of the years when they knew the joy of their own babies. There were usually honeymooners in the audience, too, equally eager to peer through the glass, looking forward perhaps to having children of their own.

We were known by many names in those days—the Dionnelles, the Quins, the Quints, *les jumelles*, the miracle babies, *les Quintuplées*. One of the names was "the five human nuggets." Now the red-roofed observatory has vanished, too. It was pulled down and its wood, to the last plank and nail, carted off to Espanola, 150 miles away, to build a house for Thérèse, our sister, who is now Mrs. Thomas Callahan.

The Big House, handsome in yellow brick and as big as a hotel, still stands on its green hill overlooking the empty road, full of every kind of memory for all of us. But Dad and Mom moved out years ago, into a new, gray bungalow that is only a fraction of its size. From their windows they can watch whoever comes and goes from the Big House. In the misty, early mornings, one can look out, too, and see deer walk delicately out of the woods and graze in the fields across the road.

Outside the Big House, a sign proclaims it to be a convalescent home. There are beds, they say, for fifty people, but there is nothing remaining to tell that this was the place where we grew up and tasted, with a sense of shock, so much of the bitterness as well as the sweetness of life. Dad did not approve of such mementos.

Much of living consists of leaving the past behind us, of thrusting it away from us so that it loses its power to dominate the present. But we always leave something of ourselves in the past. In Corbeil, where we were born, one of us will always remain, in the unkempt, lonely graveyard half a mile from the Church of the Sacred Heart of Jesus. The stone on Emilie's grave is not conspicuous, and the coarse grass grows tall around it. A stranger could scarcely find it if he tried.

There have been many times when it seemed best never to go back again to Corbeil. Finding love is not easy, and its power to heal can be slow.

In the attic of the Big House, lit by its row of dormer windows, Dad used to store his piles of newspapers. He sorted and clipped them for filing year by year in manila folders whenever they carried a story about the family that demanded his attention. His collection began with a crumbling, yellowed copy of the one newspaper he ever really trusted. *The Nugget* was and is published in North Bay, which lies a dozen miles north of Corbeil. It is a bustling town nowadays which has far outgrown the population of 23,000 people announced on the outdated roadside signs. It was our nearest shopping center, when we were permitted to shop there, the gateway to On-

13

tario's Northland with its lakes by the thousand, endless forests, and gold, silver, copper and uranium mines. But during the Depression, North Bay was close to bankruptcy.

The first copy of *The Nugget* that Dad saved was dated May 28, 1934. Probably someone gave it to him later on. It is impossible to believe he had a moment to spare that day to think about posterity. It must have been the most frantic time of his life. The newspaper reports that two Frenchmen, Rossi and Codos, had landed safely in Brooklyn after flying the Atlantic. King George V, after a long illness, was photographed riding horseback in Hyde Park, London, for the first time in two years. The weather forecast was "warm and thundery."

Across the front page, a big, black headline said "QUINTS BORN TO FARM WIFE." The importance of that event, as interpreted by *The Nugget's* editor of the day, Eddie Bunyan, was summed up in a series of other headlines: "25-year-old Corbeil Mother Establishes Canadian Mark . . . Mrs. Oliva Dionne Eligible for King's Bounty . . . Dr. A. R. Dafoe Says All Five Baby Girls Healthy . . . Weigh 13 Pounds, 6 Ounces."

There was another, secondary report headlined "Mother Will Get At Least Three Pounds," which was the amount in British money paid with the compliments of King George for a multiple birth. Mom was quoted as feeling, "Oh, pretty good." Then the reporter asked Dad, "Well, do you feel proud of yourself?"

"I'm the kind of fellow they should put in jail" was the answer. That is what *The Nugget* printed, though Dad was to overlook the lapse. He insisted, however, that he had been misunderstood and misquoted. "Our little world was entirely topsy-turvy," he said in one long letter written almost one year later, "and I knew not which way to turn for the quietness and seclusion I had

14

been accustomed to. Nurses, doctors, photographers, newspapermen and cameramen all were disturbing the peace of our home."

He decided what really happened was that a reporter for a Toronto newspaper had begun asking embarrassing questions about this overwhelming increase in the size of Dad's family. He had answered, "The way you talk, people would think I ought to be put in jail." The reporter had twisted the words, and Dad's reputation had suffered the first of what he regarded as an endless series of insults and injuries in publications around the world.

This was his way of thinking. He never spoke of the incident to us, and ours was not a family where anyone was encouraged to ask questions. The misunderstanding, if it was that, rankled with him. His relations with newspapers and newspapermen, except for *The Nugget*, were seldom good from that day on. He nourished a contempt, possibly even a fear, for them that grew rather than diminished over the years. To other people, he complained of "living in terror" of reporters and photographers when we were babies. It was their hounding of Dad and the family, he said, that drove him to lock the doors and bar the windows of the farmhouse, nail up a "No Admittance" sign and refuse to talk to strangers. We were brought up to share his feelings.

In a sense, every birth can be regarded as a miracle of survival. Every baby delivered safely into the world is one more proof of God's concern for the future of man and the happiness of women. But Mom, understandably, saw events in a different light and in a much more personal way. The birth of five daughters within the hour convinced her that this was a veritable miracle and she had been singled out for God's favor, though she would not dare, nor pretend, to understand why.

Her life up to then had not been easy. She was the only daughter in a family of seven, born in Corbeil in the house of split logs chinked with clay against the winter blizzards that her father, Moise Legros, had built with neighbors' help soon after the turn of the century. Before he was ten years old, Grandfather Legros had earned a living as a street fiddler at Masham Mills, near Ottawa, where he was born; but in Corbeil he and his family lived close to the soil as farmers, rugged, simple people, loyal to French Canada and the Catholic faith.

It was in Queen Victoria's time that the French Canadians first came from Quebec to this faraway corner of Ontario. They followed the logging camps originally, working as lumberjacks and in the sawmills. The less footloose among them took land and cleared out small fields among the outcroppings of inhospitable rock. They sent home for their families, and the settlements that sprang up knew the hardships of the frontier with its heritage of ceaseless labor. In the summer, the men scraped a living on their farms or by road work, in winter they looked to earn a few extra dollars in the lumber trade.

Grandfather Legros was working in a sawmill when he married sixteen-year-old Salomée Demers, a tall, stately girl who, to hear Mom talk about it, had the most beautiful hazel eyes for miles around. But Grandmother died at the age of thirty-three, leaving six children for Moise Legros to raise. So his only daughter, Elzire, had to leave school when she was eleven to help bring up her brothers, cooking, washing, scrubbing floors, and sewing the boys' clothes. By the time she was sixteen, with dimples in her cheeks and ribbon in her hair, she was reckoned by the neighbors to be a good catch for any young man with a mind to marry.

Dad came courting in his car—one of only two in the village in those days; the parish priest owned the other. On September 15, 1926, Oliva Dionne and Elzire Legros

16

were married in the church at Corbeil, where they had made their first Communions. She wore a white silk dress with a corsage of orange blossoms. Dad was twenty-two, Mom was six years younger. Grandfather Legros had wanted them to wait another year, but Dad must always have been a strong-willed man. In his car, they drove for their honeymoon to Ottawa, then on to Masham Mills, some fifty-five miles away. They walked through the streets where Grandfather had played his violin to coax people to throw pennies into his cap as they passed by.

The following year, she bore her first child, Ernest, alone and unattended one December night, while Dad drove a sled through five miles of drifted snow, trying to reach her grandmother, Josephat Demers, who could be depended on to know what to do in a situation like this.

Mom had five more children before us, all born in the big wooden bed that Dad's father, Olivier, brought up from Biddeford, Maine, where he had worked as a mechanic in the cotton mills of the Laconia Company. After Ernest came Rose-Marie and Thérèse. Then there was Leo, who died from pneumonia in 1930 at the age of one month; Mom used to tell us that his hair had already grown thick and curly. One year later, Daniel was born; and Pauline, the only blonde in the family, two years after that, in 1933.

All of us were delivered on that wooden bed. Under a big crucifix that hung on the wall, it filled the main bedroom in the farmhouse that opened straight off the living room. The living room, in turn, merged with the kitchen with no wall between.

The house, with its plank walls inside and out, was built by Grandfather Dionne after he came back to Ontario. He met Grandmother Rosalie Dionne when she was a weaver in the Pepperell factory in Biddeford, earning seventy-five cents a day. He was a man of fine character in every way, in the opinion of those who knew him well, some of it possibly inherited from his Scottish grandmother. For a while, before he went back to marry her, he left Rosalie behind in Biddeford, working in the mills to earn extra money while he labored singlehanded to make ready for the plow the three hundred acres he had been given as a land grant by the Crown. Corbeil possessed not so much as a name then. It was no more than a dot on the map on the main line of the Canadian Pacific Railroad, lost and anonymous in a landscape that had changed little since Samuel Champlain in 1615 voyaged up the Ottawa River and along the Mattawa to Trout Lake, then portaged across to Lake Nipissing. The old French traders came this way, gathering furs from Hurons and Algonquin. These forests were home to the *coureurs de bois*, who used to live and marry among the Indians.

There was little to distinguish the house that Grandfather built from any other of its time and place, from birch-board floors to the covered porch that ran across the front and along one side. A barn, a hayloft, a chicken house, and a tool shed clustered close, as though huddling for warmth through the long winter, when temperatures can fall to twenty and thirty below and snow banks pile up waist-high along the ice-covered roads. Then the stove, the only heat in the house, had to be stoked until it glowed to keep the cold from penetrating the uninsulated walls and roof, though in summer the place was like a furnace. In the upstairs bedrooms, two generations of Dionne children alternately shivered and sweltered their way through the seasons.

None of the rooms in the old house was a bathroom or toilet. There was no electricity or gas. Water had to be pumped from the well outside by means of the curved iron handle fixed for the purpose to the edge of the kitchen sink. By the light of smoking kerosene lamps, Mom's family was born in that house, from Ernest to the five of us. When we arrived, there was no hot-water bottle anywhere. One nurse said that the only basin to be found was the one in which the family washed.

Mom had always had more than her share of monthly pain, and her confinements were long and difficult, though the only baby she lost was Leo. A midwife attended her for Ernest and Pauline, but her three other babies were delivered by Dr. Allan Roy Dafoe, brought in from Callander. The call for the doctor, though, never went out until she was in labor; up-to-date prenatal care did not exist so far as she was concerned. Nevertheless, most of her babies were born in five hours or less, and she usually managed to be on her feet doing housework by the end of the fifth day after childbirth.

In 1934, as usual, she argued against calling the doctor in advance, though she had never felt so ill before when she was carrying a baby. She had splitting headaches, to the point where she could scarcely see. Her face was swelling up, and her hands were puffy. Her legs had swollen to twice their size. But the doctor would cost money, and Dad, through no fault of his own, was having a lean time of it.

The house and farm had not been a gift from Grandfather Dionne. Dad had bitten deep into his savings to buy the property. There was a mortgage on it that never seemed to shrink. It stood now at $3,000, which was just three times as much cash money as he had made in any of his most prosperous years from working the fields, renting out his hay-baling machine, and trapping foxes in the winter woods and selling the raw furs in North Bay.

Mom was an expert needlewoman, who could sew ten dresses in a single day if she tried. So she cut down his old suits for Ernest and made dresses from her wedding

19

trousseau for Thérèse and Rose-Marie. Dad went to work hauling gravel on the roads for the government of Ontario. He supplied his own labor, along with a wagon and two horses. While the job lasted, he was paid four dollars a day.

There were many stories in the newspapers later saying that he had been on relief for a year, like so many others around Corbeil, while a charitable agency supplied clothing for his family. It was another "wrong impression" that reporters spread about him, he used to say. He was a proud man. The idea that he could not support his own family cut him to the quick.

But Mom was certain they could not afford the doctor for her when his fee would run to twenty dollars or more. Only constant, increasing pain could have persuaded her that this time she might need help in advance from Dr. Dafoe, the shy, chubby little doctor with the scrubby mustache who lived in a brick house across the street from the Callander Hotel.

He was a widower with a single grown-up son. He lived with a housekeeper, Mrs. Little, and her daughter in a house that boasted a fine medical library and not much more than that, according to all accounts. He had never earned more than $4,500 a year, and he must have spent a fair portion of that on tobacco—his pipe was seldom out of his mouth or hand. His practice covered four hundred square miles and about 3,500 people. In the same threadbare suit and driving an old Chevrolet, he often patrolled the area in the company of a priest, one giving comfort to the soul and the other to the body, though the doctor was a Protestant and something of a fatalist, according to what we have learned subsequently.

A little more than two weeks before we arrived, Dad drove into Callander to see the doctor. Mom was so sick that she could scarcely eat. He would like some medicine for her, though he did not think it would be necessary for the doctor to call on her as yet. By everybody's reckoning, her time would not come until the end of July.

The medicine Dad took home seemed to do Mom no good. One week later, judging by tests he had made, Dr. Dafoe said that she must be put to bed immediately and a servant hired to look after the house and the children. The following day, the doctor insisted on seeing her. It had not been possible to find any household help, so she was still up and about. He ordered her to bed immediately.

She suspected that she might be carrying twins. Among her first cousins, there were three sets of them, the last, a boy and a girl, born only a few weeks earlier, and it was certainly true that some families ran to twins. The Dionnes had also produced two sets, but they were only distantly related to Dad. But Dr. Dafoe said later that he did not particularly think it was a multiple pregnancy. His diagnosis was what his profession calls a "fetal abnormality." In any event, he gave strict orders that Mom was not to be allowed out of bed, and he put her on a fluid diet. Dad reported to him twice during the next week. The swelling in her legs was disappearing, he said. The unaccustomed luxury of rest was obviously helping her.

There are many riddles in our lives. We have given up hope of ever finding full answers to some of them. Anyone who has examined the hundreds of thousands of words that were written about the events of that May 28 will perhaps wonder how there can be any mystery left. Wasn't this the most publicized birth of the century up to that time? Did any children in history arrive in the world to be nourished in such headlines and swaddled in so many acres of newsprint?

21

But the stories were told so often that they changed in the telling. The key members of the cast each abided by his own version, insisting his was the only truth. By the time we were old enough to begin to understand, truth had faded into legend and memory into myth.

⊷§ TWO ⊷

WHICH OF US was the first, and which the last, to creep into the world that May morning while dawn began to streak the sky and bird song sounded in the trees outside? Nobody knows for sure, because nobody had time to notice. "The three larger babies were born first and the two smaller ones last," Dr. Dafoe wrote in his formal report of the affair, but no one weighed or measured us with any accuracy. It is recorded, however, that for all our lack of size we could cry "fairly vigorously."

Where was Dad when Mom's labor began? She had only the older children for company. He had left for Trout Lake, a few miles away, still seeking a servant, since none had been found yet. "I'm sorry to be so late," he told Mom when he got back some time after midnight, according to a friend's account later, "but the girl already had a job in North Bay. Thought I'd never find her house, and coming home I had car trouble."

Mom's fingernails were turning blue by then. She cut short his explanation and sent him hurrying for a mid-

23

wife. Aunt Donalda lived not far down the road. At one-twenty in the morning, Dad pounded on her door. While she came over and stoked a fire in the Dionne farmhouse, he drove on to pick up Madame Benoit Lebel, an old friend of Mom's, who had eighteen children of her own and had delivered several hundred more.

By two o'clock, Dad was speeding toward Callander to warn the doctor of the emergency. Dr. Dafoe had already been called out on one obstetric case that night; during the first week of our lives, he delivered half-a-dozen other babies in Callander. It was an effort for him to rouse himself again, but he followed Dad back to Corbeil.

"I arrived," he said later, "to find the home in confusion, no preparation made for confinement, except a teakettle boiling on the stove. . . . The whole situation seemed unreal and dreamlike, but I mechanically went about the business of looking after the babies."

Two of us had arrived before him, and the first cord had been tied off by Madame Lebel with cotton thread from Mom's sewing basket. The third of us was on the way when he entered the door. He scrubbed up as best he could and took over, while the midwives scurried around looking for something to wrap us in. Dad was not in sight.

Was it Madame Legros, a Catholic, or the doctor, or both of them, who baptized us with a dipperful of water from the kitchen? It matters to no one now. What is important is that someone, with no priest there, followed the prescribed ritual, sprinkled the water and muttered, in the Latin rite, *Ego baptizo in nomine Patris et Filii et Spiritus Sancti.*

The midwives said that Mom was in a coma most of the time, but she disagreed. "I did not complain, and I did not lose consciousness," she said. "When I realized there were five of them, I was proud. But the first thing I said to Oliva was, 'What will people say when they find out about this? They will say we are pigs.' "

Meantime, we had been wrapped in the only coverings to be found, remnants of cotton sheets and old napkins. We were laid on a corner of Grandfather's bed, covered with a blanket that had been heated at the stove. The doctor doubted that any of us would survive.

Mom suddenly went into shock, her pulse fluttering and temperature falling fast. She was given injections and warmed with blankets, but to Dr. Dafoe she looked like a dying woman. Dad was still missing. As the only one with a car, the doctor hurried away to fetch Father Daniel Routhier to administer the last rites. The Corbeil priest, who lived nearly three miles off, was an old friend of the family, a talkative, lean little man whom Dad liked well enough. One of our brothers had been named for him.

While the doctor was away, Mom's condition took a decided turn for the better, though the hemorrhaging had not stopped. Father Routhier anointed her and administered Extreme Unction, but two hours later she was out of danger. She had been thinking not of death but of poverty. "Five," she kept saying. "How will we clothe so many children?"

One of the midwives went over to a neighbor's for something to put us in. It was an ordinary wicker basket such as butchers use. Heated blankets were folded into it, then we were placed in a row inside and covered with another blanket warmed at the stove. In a little while, we were carried to the kitchen itself and set by the stove's open door for extra heat, while the midwives took us briefly out, one by one, for a gentle massage with warm olive oil.

Dad seems to have been fascinated by the arithmetic of the situation. In the attic of the Big House, he saved accounts of multiple births, perhaps as consolation for

25

the trouble we caused him. He discovered that in fathering five babies at once he was a man in approximately 57 million. That made him a person of very special distinction, and he was not inclined to forget it. The exact odds were calculated by some experts as 57,289,761 to 1. To this day, the statistics have a strange appeal for some of our friends and family, though it is not easy to understand why.

By one expert's count, we were the thirty-fourth case that could be authenticated for medical history, but there were undoubtedly others that were not reported. The first records date back to 1694, according to Dad's files, and the closest at hand, before the Dionnes, to 1923. Quintuplets were born in Lisbon, Portugal, in 1866 and in Kentucky thirty years after. In 1914, an Italian mother, Rose Salemi, gave birth to five babies, in 1943 the Diligenti quintuplets were born in Argentina, and in a single week in September, 1963, the five Prieto boys were born in Venezuela and four girls and a boy to Mrs. Andrew Fischer of Aberdeen, South Dakota.

Doctors found that twins are born in every eighty-seven confinements, triplets in every 7,569. That is the mathematical square of 87, or so the experts say. Arithmetic is not a subject in which any of us excelled in school, so we can only quote the mathematicians. Multiply 7,569 by 87 and you arrive at the figure for quadruplets: 658,503. Multiplying that by the mysterious 87 produces 57,289,761. And there we should prefer to leave it. There is no great joy in regarding ourselves, or being regarded, as arithmetical freaks of nature.

For the time being, we were evidently that, and little more than that, to Dr. Dafoe. He had the reputation for being exceedingly well read in medical affairs, through his books and his piles of doctors' magazines, though he was only a country doctor who in winter had to travel by horse-drawn sleigh to reach some of his patients. He kept abreast of the latest developments in his profession, and he had a good idea of the chances of survival for quintuplets: the odds were impossible, according to everything he knew. Yet he was obviously a man whose mind was receptive to fresh ideas, who would try anything that common sense suggested. This was proved time and again in his early care for us. He had more than a little personal courage, too. As a diabetic himself, he lived on a tightrope, dependent on the injections of insulin he had to administer to himself every day. But this was a secret in those days.

In his diary, he tersely noted the birth of "5F." He apparently held out little hope that we would live. Madame Lebel remembered that he told her, "There isn't much anybody can do. Maybe the first baby will live until tomorrow, but the others will probably be dead before night."

He spoke in English, of course, because like the majority of people in the area he spoke only a few words of French. The forecast he made to Madame Lebel became part of the heritage of animosity that sprang up between him and our family. He died after a long and painful illness before our tenth birthday, when the old intimacy with him had been destroyed, so there was no opportunity for us to know him as a man or try to find answers to some of the questions in our hearts. But his actions after he left the farmhouse did not indicate a total lack of hope for us.

Early that morning Uncle Leon, Dad's oldest brother, who ran a garage in Callander, drove out to Dad's barn to collect manure for his garden. The doctor saw him there and went out to give him the first, unbelievable news of how he had delivered five new nieces as morning had dawned. Uncle Leon decided it was a great joke and headed back to Callander. The doctor hurried in to take another look at Mom before he too drove home. He left no special instructions for our care. For the first twenty-four hours, we were to be given nothing but a few drops of sweetened water from an eyedropper every two hours.

In Callander, Dr. Dafoe stopped off at the post office to pick up his mail. He told Mrs. Tate, the postmistress, that he had just seen five babies into the world. On a street corner outside, he stopped Grandfather Dionne and gave him the news of his five extra granddaughters. Grandfather immediately had the same anxious thought that leaped instinctively into the minds of everyone around us: "How will my son take care of all those children?" It was inconceivable that he could afford us. There was not enough money to provide for quintuplets.

That day, Dr. Dafoe took time to drive the ten miles to Bonfield and the Red Cross post there. He asked the nurse on duty, Miss Cloutier, to call at the farmhouse as soon as she could, more for the sake of Mom than for us. Would she please do her best to help? Then she was to report back to him at his surgery on the ground floor of his little brick house. He himself went on his daily rounds, over the miles of scattered farms and farmhouses hidden among the forests and fields. At home, the midwives continued to keep watch over Mom and her older children.

It was not the doctor who spread the word that brought about the invasion of reporters, photographers, curiosity seekers and sensation mongers that very shortly turned our village into a madhouse. Just before eight o'clock, Uncle Leon telephoned Eddie Bunyan at *The Nugget*. As a joke, he asked, "Does a birth notice for five cost more than a regular advertisement?"

The editor kept him talking long enough to ferret out the facts, then sent a reporter and a photographer, Dick Railton, hurrying down to Corbeil. In his office, Bunyan wound a sheet of copy paper into his typewriter and began to rattle out the bulletin that put us under the microscope of mankind's inquisitive wonder: "Mrs. Oliva Dionne gave birth to five girls today . . ."

Those were the first words of the millions that were written about us in the course of the years that followed. Almost instantly, the advance guard of newspapermen and photographers was hurrying north to Corbeil. There were kindly instincts at work and a realization of our family's needs. One of the first out-of-town newspapermen to reach the scene brought an old-fashioned incubator. Another, Keith Munro, who at one time became our "manager," turned up with three hundred dollars' worth of equipment, including twelve dozen sorely needed diapers and a small bathtub.

It fell to us to have our first photograph taken when we were only a few hours old. When the two men from *The Nugget* arrived at the farmhouse, we were lifted out of our nest of blankets in the meat basket in the kitchen and tucked into bed beside Mom, with only five faces the size of apples showing, for a birthday portrait by flash bulb.

Dad had appeared on the scene and, by all accounts, was close to hysteria. He had not slept all night and had not thought to shave. His thick, dark hair was uncombed, his eyes were tense, his lean face was gray with fatigue and concern. His workaday clothes were crumpled, and he wore no tie. The photographers snapped that picture too, and it was distributed around the world, creating an impression of Dad that never matched the truth.

Mom was still in dire need of expert medical care. Pauline, still a baby herself, lay in her crib in the big downstairs room of the house. The other children were scampering in and out, excited by all the fuss. The place must have been like an oven that sultry, thundery morning, with the stove in the kitchen kept glowing red to warm us. The midwives carefully doled out the sweetened water from the eyedropper to feed us.

Nurse Cloutier had called, concentrated her examination on Mom and reported to the doctor that in her opinion it was essential to put a trained nurse in charge on a round-the-clock basis. The doctor set out immediately to find one. The girl he engaged was Yvonne Leroux, the twenty-year-old daughter of Georges, who ran one of Callander's two taxis and lived two doors away from Dr. Dafoe. She had just graduated from St. Joseph's Hospital in North Bay, and we were to be her first outside case. She will always have a special place in our memories from the years she spent looking after us. Because it seemed that Dad could not afford to pay her, Dr. Dafoe guaranteed her salary so that she would agree to come to us.

She arrived for duty that afternoon. She brought her own hot-water bottle, which made it easier to keep up a steady temperature in the meat basket. The doctor came back that evening, and what he saw astonished him. Mom was still feverish but on the way to recovery. Her daughters were still breathing, though at times the breaths would almost stop, before they picked up and raced along at twice the normal speed.

Since then, there have been many turns to our lives, some for better, some for worse, but this was the first. It marked a corner turned and a slim chance that we might perhaps survive. Suddenly all manner of things began to happen.

Nurse Leroux began keeping medical records on the case. Without any proper charts, she used a wad of billheads from Dan J. Saya's drugstore, which used to stand at No. 98 Main Street in North Bay ("sheet music and records always carried in stock," the billheads said). The history of those times, painstakingly written out in a young girl's neat hand week by week, still exists in the files of Dr. William A. Dafoe, our Dr. Dafoe's younger brother. It tells of Mom's slow recovery from her ordeal, complicated by anemia and phlebitis in her right leg, of her being allowed up, but then being returned to bed some two weeks later. It hints, too, at the ceaseless struggle that was necessary for the survival of five wrinkled, blue-skinned little creatures with spidery limbs.

On the second day, we were moved into roomier quarters, when the meat basket was exchanged for a laundry basket. Some more hot-water bottles were rounded up, replacing the heated bricks and old-fashioned flatirons that had previously been folded into the blankets surrounding us. We had to be watched every minute. Many times during the day and night, the nurse had to rouse one after the other of us, as the sparks of life seemed to fade. Her only sleep was to doze now and then in a chair. It was a harassing introduction to nursing for Yvonne Leroux.

Mom had never been able to nurse her babies for more than a few days in the best of times. Now a new problem was growing more acute hour by hour: how were we to be fed? After twenty-four hours, the doctor instructed Nurse Leroux to start us on a seven-twenty formula of cow's milk and boiled water, with two spoonfuls of corn syrup added from the can on the kitchen shelf, and one or two drops of rum as a stimulant. This was to be served every two hours around the clock.

Other doctors used to ask Dr. Dafoe why he prescribed rum instead of the more customary brandy. "I couldn't afford brandy," he told them. "Rum is cheaper and it works just as well."

A few, more prominent physicians became disturbed about the publicity he was being given in the newspapers, which were busy building up the legends surrounding Corbeil, the Dionnes and the "little doc." The flood of stories about him were unethical and undignified, these other doctors complained. There were rumors that efforts had been made to keep the reporter with the incubator, an American from Chicago, out of Canada, and even when he was allowed in, he had to pay duty on his gift.

Meanwhile, Dr. Dafoe had a more urgent problem. He combed the neighborhood looking for nursing mothers who might be able to provide breast milk. The supply was meager, but what little was obtained was poured into the seven-twenty mixture. The problem soon solved itself. Supplies were on the way. That was pledged in one of the hundreds of calls that kept his telephone ringing as soon as the story of "the miracle of Corbeil" was told in the newspapers and in radio bulletins.

Four days later, breast milk arrived first from Chicago, then from the Sick Children's Hospital in Toronto and the Royal Victoria Hospital in Montreal. Given by mothers of every class and kind, it alone was used, full strength, to feed us. We owe so much to so many people. How many hundreds of women helped to nurse us, we can never know. There is a story that Negro mothers contributed to those critical days. It is still spoken of in whispers by some in Corbeil, as though it were a kind of scandal. We do not think so. Gratitude knows no such bounds of prejudice.

For the first days of our lives, it was uncertain what help, if any, might come from the outside world that lay so far in miles and understanding from our village. The question that made it impossible for Dad to think with his usual clarity was, *Who will pay for all this?* There was no joy for him in our birth, and only a tiny crumb of it later. There may have been some stirring of pride, but the harsh truth appeared to be that he would, at last, have to go looking for charity.

The first gift that had arrived was a package from the Women's Institute of Callander containing medical supplies and a roll of flannelette. Because Mom's time had come two months early, she had nothing ready, none of the things she usually loved to make in advance during her pregnancies. The flannelette provided our first clothing.

There had been no scales in the house and none in the village small enough to weigh us separately, but on the second day a scoop scale was borrowed so that a beginning could be made in the keeping of records. Together, it was found, we amounted to 13 pounds 6 ounces, before we were returned to the laundry basket. The next day, the three smallest—whoever of us they might have been—were moved into a safer sanctuary—the first incubator, which arrived with the reporter from Chicago.

It was an old-fashioned model, heated with hot water in a copper tank, the only kind that would be of any service in our old home. It was made with a hinged glass top and was equipped with a holder for a sponge, which was soaked in hot water to keep the humidity high, and a thermometer, which usually stood at ninety degrees. There was room inside it for only three, so the other two of us stayed on in the laundry basket until the end of the week, when a second incubator was presented to us. This was a different type, heated by earthenware containers which came to be known as "little pigs." Later on, three more incubators were constructed, giving each of us snug quarters of her own.

But none of this evidence of the world's generosity had come to hand to ease Dad's mind when he put on his hat and went to see Father Routhier. He needed help—down-to-earth material help—for his family, now that the routine of their lives was broken and debts appeared to be piling up on every side. The priest promised to collect what he could from his congregation. He would call on his handful of parishioners for whatever help they might be able to spare.

33

He could not have encouraged Dad to expect much. This was a poor parish in an impoverished area of Ontario, in a world where prosperity, by and large, was only a dream of the past and a hope for the future. Local farmers could not sell what their fields grew or their herds produced. Father Routhier was forced to say Mass in a basement because there was no money for building a church. It was built later, when we were children and money had flowed into the district. Mom donated the lamp in the sanctuary.

Callander itself, though bigger than Corbeil, was not much more than an abandoned lumber town. Four of its five lumber mills had burned down and had not been rebuilt. The one that was left was closed. Summers brought in a few visitors from more prosperous parts of Canada, to rent cottages and houseboats on the shore of Lake Nipissing, like those owned by Leo Kervin, a lifelong friend of Dad's. But beyond that there was not much money coming in for anyone.

The railroad station had been destroyed by fire and had never been replaced. Instead, an old boxcar with a pot-bellied stove was used to accommodate the handful of passengers who traveled on the line. The Callander Hotel, where lumberjacks had once stomped their boots on the pine boards and splashed their dollars around, was a shabby relic of its gaudier days, as bare of fresh paint as most of the other buildings. In the township surrounding Callander, it was a rare householder who could scrape up enough even to pay his taxes. A plot of land could be bought, if anyone had the money, for two hundred dollars. There were eight hundred people on relief.

We have sometimes talked among ourselves about which of the three great virtues overshadows the rest—Faith, Hope or Charity. Annette usually votes for Faith, Cécile for Hope, Marie and Yvonne for Charity as the supreme virtue, which is what the Bible says. Father Routhier could find little charity in Corbeil that season of 1934, and who is to be blamed for that?

The Dionne Quintuplets were creatures of the times. The Depression had brought anxiety and hardship to all but a few specially privileged people. In every corner of the world, factories had closed their gates, and the unemployed were to be counted by the millions. Trade was at a standstill, and farmers were compelled to plough their crops back into the good earth that had grown them. It was an era when famine flourished in the midst of plenty; and we were a kind of antidote, it seems. Without knowing the least thing about it, we were able to contribute something toward helping the world make light of its problems. All those pictures, thousands and thousands of them, of five laughing children without a care served as a kind of fairy tale for grownups, a fantasy of an earthly paradise where everyone could be happy, where the sun always shone and nobody knew the meaning of hunger or grief.

It is impossible, though, not to wonder how our lives might have been changed if times had been easier, if the parishioners of Father Routhier had been able to spare a mite of charity for Mom and Dad so that he would not have felt compelled to put his need for money ahead of our need for love.

As it was, he was at his wits' end, not knowing where to turn. After he left the priest and drove home, a crowd of strangers had gathered on the road outside the farmhouse, the first of the thousands who swarmed into the village to see what all the excitement was about. The family was rapidly becoming celebrated, which did not please Dad at all. The fate of five babies was beginning to intrigue newspaper readers and radio listeners everywhere.

We had another session with a photographer, and our

first interview with Keith Munro, of the *Toronto Star*. "There was something terribly exciting about those babies that made thrills run up and down my spine," he said later. "I can't explain it, but I've seen it happen to other people."

He held the flash equipment while the photographer clicked away with the camera. We had all been popped into bed beside Mom. The first two flash bulbs were fired without any trouble. But the third exploded and showered the bedroom with splinters of glass. Apparently Mom and Dr. Dafoe, who was there to supervise, did not object; but for the next shots, every bulb was carefully wrapped up in a handkerchief.

Enough was enough, though, and the doctor ordered that no more pictures were to be taken by other cameramen. He asked Grandfather Dionne to stand guard, with a pitchfork, to keep the house secure against reporters and the thousands of sightseers who were flocking to Corbeil like moths drawn by a candle flame.

"We're tired of all the visitors," Grandfather grumbled. "It's hard to know whom to trust. I guess it's best not to trust anybody." How typical that was of our family.

Dad and the doctor were alike in those early days in resenting the gale winds of publicity that brought the sightseers to Corbeil. Both felt that strangers were intruding into their private affairs. In the end, the doctor had a change of heart and wrote, "I came to realize that I had no right to object to what had become a matter of continent-wide interest. I have been increasingly grateful to the newspapers for the invaluable supplies and equipment which from the beginning came as a result of this publicity."

Dad did not see it that way at all. "We were pointedly told the press had power to make or break a man," he declared later. "It chose to make Dr. Dafoe and break us, to serve its own ends."

He came close to trusting one stranger who had heard about the Quints. His name was Ivan I. Spear, and he lived in Chicago—which happened to be the source of so many things good and bad for us. He operated the Century of Progress Tour Bureau, and he sensed at once that there were great commercial possibilities in this once-in-57-million-times affair. What a tourist attraction we could be turned into! Acting immediately, he placed a telephone call to Uncle Leon, who was listed in the directories, to see what chance there was of signing the Quints to appear as a side-show attraction at the Chicago World's Fair, which had opened just one year earlier.

The majority of people are fortunate in that they grow up in oblivion about the circumstances of their birth and the most tender years of childhood. There are the reminiscences of their family, mellowed by the years, and the snapshots in the family album; there is usually no more than that, and a little of the wonder of each birth remains as an inheritance for each individual. It is different with ourselves. So many words, so many pictures survive that one is at a loss to interpret them. For years, when we had grown well beyond the age of reason and were assumed to have acquired the sense of right and wrong, we knew nothing of Ivan Spear. What we know now is from hearsay and at second hand. In our family, it is forbidden to pry into the Chicago contract that was signed with Mr. Spear.

A go-between persuaded Dad that he ought to consider the offer to put us on exhibition. There would be trained nurses to watch over us, Dad was told, and we should certainly be cared for better than at home, in a kind of luxurious private ward with windows through which the spectators could peer in at us. All this would be guaranteed. Dad, it is said, needed other opinions before he made up his mind. This surely has the ring of truth. He likes to turn any question over and over in his mind, searching for flaws, avoiding hasty decisions like the plague. He turned first to Dr. Dafoe and drove to Callander to seek his advice.

A doctor by training and necessity must often make quick decisions. In our family, the accepted version of their meeting is that the doctor told Dad, "Yes, go get all the money you can. They're going to die, anyway, and they may as well die in Chicago as die here." Dad has often quoted those words in justification of what was done. Were they ever actually spoken? Who can tell? We have learned that Dr. Dafoe was a fatalist who disliked taking the initiative. He was exhausted by the responsibilities that our birth had piled on his shoulders. But his brother, Dr. William, has said that the cynicism of those words was utterly uncharacteristic of him. And little more than one year later, Dr. Dafoe had called us "the greatest pleasure of my life."

When Dad went on to discuss the proposed contract with Father Routhier, the priest did not argue against it. Instead, as adviser and manager, he rode out with Dad in Georges Leroux's taxi for a rendezvous with Ivan Spear and the promoter's attorney. The chosen site for their meeting was Orillia, because there was a landing field there and Mr. Spear had flown up from Chicago, so urgent was the business in hand. Orillia is 160 miles from Corbeil. The meeting and its purpose could supposedly be kept a secret.

We were three days old when Dad signed the contract to put us on show to the Century of Progress. His signature made him an employee of Mr. Spear's at an immediate salary of $100 and expenses, which was to be increased to $250 when we arrived for exhibition. In return, the promoter had been granted "exclusive rights to pictures of the five infant daughters, newspaper pictures and movies; and to all advertising contracts that might be obtained for and with the children."

Mr. Spear's organization would collect 70 per cent of the profits earned by the sideshow. Dad would have 23 per cent. The remaining 7 per cent was to be Father Routhier's share, a contribution toward building the new church that was needed so badly. That first Sunday, he preached a sermon about us in the basement that served as his church. Our birth was a challenge indeed, he said.

The contract that Dad signed did not in any sense deliver us to the mercies of the World's Fair or its promoters. Paragraph Ten of the document—copies still exist—stipulated that the Tour Bureau "will exhibit the employee and his family under conditions and medical supervision acceptable to the physician in charge of the mother and the Quintuplets." Another clause gave the doctor the final word on when we might be bundled off to Chicago. We were to go, it said, "at the direction of the Tour Bureau at the earliest date the physician in charge of the babies decides they can be moved without possibility of injurious effect." Dad collected $100 in advance from Mr. Spear, and Georges Leroux's taxi made for home.

Over these past months, we have dwelt much in the past. It has not been altogether a pleasant experience. After nearly thirty years, as this is written, the past has not lost its power to hurt. What were the real feelings in Dad's heart when he put his name to the contract? Did he act only for money, with his eyes closed to all other considerations, or was there a glimmering of love for us? Was the day's work done with regret for its necessity or with relief that there was money in his pocket at last? If he believed that we should die, how much did he care?

He has never answered these unspoken questions, and up to now none of us has dared to ask them of him. But

39

some day one of us will surely have the courage. It will be better then for all of us.

In what he has said and written for publication, he makes little of the matter. "It was not long until I discovered that the contract wasn't legal. It did not have my wife's signature, so it did not give me concern." He returned the hundred dollars.

In the ignorance of the ways of worldly men that Dad and the priest and the doctor shared, they did not imagine that news of the deal would be published. In fact, Mr. Spear announced his enterprise to the newspapers soon after Georges Leroux had turned his taxi around and left Orillia.

The story made more headlines, as everything concerning the Quintuplets seemed to. The headlines started people in the Ontario government wondering what should be done to prevent heedless men from furthering their own ends at the expense of the Dionnes. Those headlines resulted, two months later, in Dad and Mom losing us, in our growing up away and apart from them.

~§ THREE §~

OUTSIDE THE FARMHOUSE there were crowds, and inside there was congestion and overcrowding to the point where the rooms must have threatened to burst their plank walls. By the end of the fifth day, the number of people wholly engaged in caring for us had increased to five, not counting the doctor or Mom, who was still confined to bed. We had been moved into a little back room next to hers, with a hole cut in the partition between, so that she could see us.

An uncle of ours, Leon Demers, had come to serve as an orderly, with his work cut out to keep the fire blazing in the stove, to make certain that the incubators stayed at close to 90 degrees, and to help with the mountains of laundry. An aunt, Laurence Clusiaux, served as cook-general and housekeeper. A second nurse had joined Yvonne Leroux, and then the redoubtable Madame Louise de Kiriline arrived, determined to bring order out of chaos.

She had been on leave in Toronto from the Red Cross post at Bonfield when Dr. Dafoe telephoned her. She immediately drove five hours nonstop to be by his side. She recalled the moment that she walked through our front door, whose glass panels must have shown a scene of such confusion that only a heart as sturdy as hers could fail to be daunted. "I heard a sound like the mewing of very feeble, very new kittens," she said. "Yes, they were alive. But that was about all."

She was acquainted with the house. She had visited there when Thérèse was a baby. Now Madame de Kiriline, on the doctor's word, was the "Number Two Boss," while he was "Number One." She made a lasting impression on everyone who met her, including us, though she disappeared from our lives when we were very young. We have misty memories of her, with her hollow cheeks, strong white teeth and a little white cap perched on her dark hair. She believed firmly in "laws and principles" in raising us, and she was a strict disciplinarian.

She swept like a whirlwind into the cluttered farmhouse. War was declared simultaneously on insects, dirt and disorder. She scrubbed and disinfected everything from floor to ceiling. She pried open nailed-up windows and tacked netting to deter the biting black flies and mosquitoes that swarmed around the barns in hot weather. She hung sheets across the open doorway of the improvised nursery where the incubators stood, to emphasize the need for seclusion and the rule that hospital gowns and masks must be worn by everyone who entered.

Later, looking back with a thought for what might have been, she confessed that in concentrating so fiercely on us, she overlooked the effect on Mom and Dad. They felt that she was an arrogant taskmistress. They came to resent her almost as much as they resented Dr. Dafoe, and for the same bewildering blend of reasons.

The veranda of the house was forever strung with diapers, eighty of them to be washed every day. Inside, the place was crammed with the five older children, sterilizers, washing machines, feeding bottles, the incubators, scales and the hundred other items indispensable to a nursery for five. There were the gas cylinders too, with their mixture of oxygen and a dash of carbon dioxide which had been imported, replacing the rum rations as the best means of stimulating us when breathing grew weak. We were given a few minutes with the inhalator before each feeding as what the doctor called our *apéritif*. The gas was used until we were three months old, fourteen cylinders of it in all, a total of 1,120 gallons. "It was most interesting and very satisfying to watch how the gas would stir up these torpid little babies and produce an energetic sucking from the Breck feeders," the doctor noted.

Mom would occasionally slip out of bed into the nursery to murmur a prayer over us and sometimes sprinkle the incubators with holy water. We were lifted out only once a day, for the nurses to give us oil baths. That went on for two months, then soap and water replaced the baby oil.

The first week had brought some minor crises. The usual loss of weight in newly born babies had taken us down below a total of less than ten pounds, and Marie to only twenty-four ounces. On the fifth day three of us had become what the records describe as "markedly distended" after forty-eight hours of constipation. The doctor administered a saline solution with a hypodermic syringe fitted with a rubber tube.

Nurse Leroux was terrified. "Doctor, it will kill them," she is reported to have said.

"If it isn't done, they will die for sure," was his reply. We were rewarded with a few drops of rum, and "they seemed to pick up and took their food better," as he recorded the rather delicate maneuver later. Each feeding at that time amounted to less than one ounce apiece.

The first week was obviously the most challenging for everyone around us. By the time the second week had come and gone, the initial shock of our arrival had begun to ease. We were gradually being accepted, more or less, as a condition of life for all those who had taken on the burden of caring for us. Dr. Dafoe took advantage of the comparative calm to organize his forces for the battles of tomorrow.

Our five brothers and sisters were moved out of the house to stay with relatives, since some of them showed signs of bronchitis and the doctor wanted no risks to be run of our catching it from them. The nurses made themselves busy—as if there were not enough to do—sewing layettes, consisting of little sleeveless dresses, jackets of cotton gauze, cotton mouth wipes and custom-tailored diapers of smaller-than-usual proportions. On those *apéritifs* of oxygen and carbon dioxide, we were all noticeably gaining weight.

Dr. William Dafoe, who practiced in Toronto and lectured in the Department of Obstetrics and Gynecology of the university there, had driven up to Callander to confer with his brother. They began talking at nine o'clock one evening and went on talking until four the following morning. Every detail of the birth and plans for our survival were discussed while Dr. Roy's memory of the events was sharp and clear. He had the workaday wisdom of years of rural practice, Dr. William had expert, scholastic knowledge.

In Ottawa, the capital city of the Dominion of Canada, the conviction was growing that something would have to be done about the Dionnes, and done in a hurry. The scare stories about the World's Fair contract had made sure of that. In North Bay an emergency committee had been set up to keep track of the situation itself and of the supplies and equipment that were pouring in. The chairman of that committee was a Red Cross inspector, William H. Alderson, who filed his reports with the Attorney General of the province, Arthur Roebuck.

It was decided that the only way to protect the Quintuplets from exploitation in side shows and from similar hazards was to appoint a board of guardians. Toward the end of July, temporary guardians had been appointed. Over Mom's protests and tears, we were put under their care. We were to become special wards of King George V of England, in the guardians' custody, when "An Act for the Protection of the Dionne Quintuplets" was passed by the Ottawa government the following March.

Dad and Mom did not appear at the North Bay courthouse on the appointed day to sign their assent to our being placed in the board's custody. To show their disapproval of the whole proceeding, they stayed away. It was the first of many similar absences, not forgetting our own first birthday party.

Across the road from the farmhouse, a swarm of workmen began putting in the stone foundations for a brandnew home for the Quintuplets. A Red Cross fund-raising drive had produced the money. In this new, nine-room nursery, we were to have electricity, central heating, plumbing and every imaginable comfort. Each of us would have a separate cot, now that we had graduated from incubators, in a big, well-aired room where the sunlight streamed in, morning and afternoon.

A well was drilled and a septic tank was installed. Power was brought in by a cable specially laid from the main highway, and Dad was allowed to hook up to it and bring electricity into the old house for the first time, too. A separate two-story building was put up to replace the tents in which the nurses had been living, for want of room for them in the farmhouse. The staff house, as it was called, was divided in two, one half for the three nurses, the other for the three policemen who had been assigned the job of guarding us. The rest of the ever-expanding staff, one housekeeper and two maids, lived in the main building with us.

Dad and Mom watched from an upstairs window in the farmhouse while the masons and carpenters and plumbers and painters went about their work on the seven acres of our new estate. The two of them stayed home when Madame de Kiriline and Miss Leroux laid the cornerstone, but Mom slipped Sacred Heart medals inside the walls of the main building before it was completed.

The new buildings, all of redwood in keeping with the local style, were surrounded by a steel-mesh fence seven feet tall, topped with barbed wire. The land, studded with outcroppings of rock, sloped down toward the road, which was rebuilt at this time to give the tourists a smooth run when they came to see us. There was a little flower garden within the fence, trees, patches of cultivated lawn and a whole colony of birdhouses for the luckiest members of our community, who could fly over the fence whenever they pleased.

One more crisis was to be endured before the move into our bright new home took place. It seems that the diapers that had been so carefully cut to our dimensions had been improperly sterilized. In any case, each of us in turn developed alarming symptoms, with soaring temperatures, racing pulses and total irresponsibility at one end. We had all been more or less anemic, but now this grew worse, and the doctor added an iron mixture to our diet.

But it was doubtful whether this alone would do to correct the anemia. Dr. Dafoe prepared to give us blood transfusions. Tests showed that we were all type O. The doctor, with his brother's help, found prospective donors, outside our own family, but chance kept him from actually carrying out the procedure. In those days, the medical profession thought that so long as the donor's blood type was the same as the patient's, all was well. The factor of incompatibility, named Rh for the rhesus monkeys who were the guinea pigs in the experiments which disclosed the danger, had not been discovered. There was a risk, unknown to Dr. Dafoe, that transfusions would have brought the "miracle of Corbeil" to a sudden conclusion.

The move into the new hospital-nursery took place on a chilly, wet day toward the end of September. Fall comes early in northern Ontario, and people who remember the day say there had already been a frost. The work of building was not quite finished, and the nurses slept on mattresses on the floor for the first few nights. But the five of us had colds, with temperatures past the 100-degree mark. Dr. Dafoe wanted us out of the drafty farmhouse, so that he might now have what he called the "opportunity for unrestricted medical control in the care of the babies."

A car took us the hundred or so yards from one door to the other. In it sat the doctor with Marie, bundled in blankets in his arms. Nurse Leroux carried Yvonne, and Madame de Kiriline, Annette. The housekeeper, Laurence Clusiaux, brought Cécile, and Emilie was on the unaccustomed lap of Lias Legros, Mom's brother and our godfather. Not long after we had been tucked into the brand-new cots, so the story goes, the heating system went awry, and a plumber had to be brought in a hurry.

It is impossible to draw sharp lines to mark the frontier between things which one only imagines can be remembered and those events which are really stored away in memory. We have read a great deal about the beginning of this chapter in our lives. At some point along the way—sooner, it seems, rather than later—the first, faint, personal recollections stir in the mind. We moved forward out of inert babyhood into a wonderful world of childhood.

We lived in our hospital-nursery, surrounded originally by the one steel-mesh fence to keep the crowds at a distance, and then by a second fence, when the first was deemed inadequate. It was possible now to be introduced to fresh air and sunshine, where previously we had been confined permanently indoors.

For the sake of the thousands of people who streamed to Corbeil, the nurses began to exhibit the Quints, holding us up one by one, with a card to tell which of us was on view. Sometimes only the card was changed and the same baby shown as though she were one of her sisters, but only the nurses knew that secret, of course, and the crowd was well satisfied.

On fine days, we were carried up and down the open porch that ran on two sides of the main building. That first winter, wrapped up to the eyes against the dry cold, we spent hours outdoors. It was a novel idea, so far as the village was concerned, to put babies out in such weather, when the majority of families stayed as close as possible to the kitchen stove and sealed the windows with rags and gummed paper against drafts. But to judge by all the records, we thrived on this carefully controlled exposure. "These happy little souls soon took on the rotund appearance of little puppies," the doctor wrote in a tribute to our health, if not to our appearances.

He resented the idea—somebody was always resenting something—that we were being "exhibited." He rationalized: "When you know people have driven thousands of miles for a glimpse of them, it is hard to see visitors go away disappointed." On the other hand, to Dad's way of thinking, the porch shows were a scandal, and we were being "theatricalized" as we learned to wave and throw kisses to our audience or play pat-a-cake with the nurses.

Thousands of people who either saw or read about us felt compelled to write to the doctor, offering their help or advice on how to raise five babies simultaneously. It

48

was a subject on which anyone could be an expert, or at least a pioneer. Letters came from all over North America, from Great Britain, Germany, France, Australia, India, Mexico, the Philippines.

Nursing mothers applied for jobs. Farmers offered their prize cows, goats and even pigs, as the healthiest, most dependable milk supply for us. Astrologers were heard from, as well as Christian Scientists, chiropractors and veterinarians. There were recommendations for every conceivable medication and for some inconceivable ones, including watermelon juice, blackberry root, sassafras and knotweed. The files contain one treasured letter that reads:

DEAR SIR,

I notice by the evening paper that you are waiting on a lady who is mother of five baby girls. You sure have your hands full. What carries away babies is Diareh or summer complaint or looseness of the bowels. Now the best cure I know is perfectly harmless.

Get pure Rye Whiskey and pour one teaspoon into a saucer. Take a clean pine sliver and set it on fire until it goes out. The dose for a medium cized baby (5–6 lbs) would be i drop every 2 hrs. There ain't no poison in pure Rye Whiskey after it is burnt, and I am anxious to see you pull through with them all. This is why I am putting you on to this cure.

From the time we were two months old, we had been receiving vitamin D, and by the following spring we were swallowing two drams of cod-liver oil each every day. Vitamin C came from orange juice, beginning with half an ounce and increasing to three or four ounces. We were taken off breast milk soon after the move into the nursery, and a mixture of cow's milk, water and Dextri-

Maltose was substituted for it. Yet, oddly enough in that farming community, the cow's milk was found to be undependable, so evaporated milk in cans was used in its place.

Our diet followed the classic pattern for babies. Prune juice was introduced on October 12, according to the records, Pablum on October 26. Strained vegetables made their appearance on January 5, followed by egg yolk one week later. On January 19, along came the first spoonfuls of cooked fruit pulp, apples, apricots and prunes. The weight charts soared up in five almost unwavering lines.

We were weighed, measured, tested, studied and examined to the heart's content of doctors and scientists, who apparently found us to be among the most fascinating females known to history. The three nurses were responsible for keeping up one of the most complete record systems ever devised. In the gentlest possible fashion, we were peered at, pricked and prodded for years. Footprints were taken, along with fingerprints. Our blood was grouped, our skulls and ears measured in millimeters. Every mouthful of food was counted, as well as every diaper.

The doctors concluded that we were, beyond doubt, identical in origin, created from a single egg cell, nourished before birth from a single placenta. The egg cell had twinned once to produce Yvonne and Annette. Then it had twinned again to produce Cécile together with another egg, from which Emilie and Marie grew.

Among ourselves, there was obviously never any question about who was whom from the moment that we could sense ourselves to be individuals. We could not understand how anyone could be so foolish as to mistake one for another, though that constantly happened when people came to call on us. It was not always possible to resist the temptation to add to the confusion when visitors called, invariably in the white gowns that the doctor insisted upon for years. Emilie, for instance, might announce herself to be Annette, or Cécile might say blandly, "I'm Yvonne."

The geneticists reported that any two of us proved as much alike as identical twins. The blood group was the same: O. The eyes were all the same, medium brown flecked with gray, though Mom decided privately that only Cécile's were exactly like those of Grandmother Legros, long since dead. Four of us had suspicions that Cécile was always favored by Mom on that account.

There was something else we had in common. Between the second and third toes on each of ten feet there is what doctors call "a mild form of syndactyly." In plainer language, it is a scarcely noticeable membrane of thin skin, a condition sometimes found in identical twins. It must run in the family in some manner. Claude, who is Cécile's oldest son, was born with exactly the same distinguishing mark.

The investigators continued to scrutinize us from top to toe. They made plaster casts of our hands and feet. Dad helped them one day and was fascinated to see how quickly the plaster hardened. As each of us submitted to the process, eager to obey the stern instruction not to move for a whole twenty seconds, the other four were allowed to watch.

Our eyes were tested, and our ears and noses. One of the countless charts gravely noted that eyelashes were "long, curled, dark brown," that the hair form was "wavy" and the skin color "light and fair." During one wintertime session, we were all X-rayed, joint by joint, and considered, reassuringly, to be "within the range of normal."

Today, we can find some reward in all the probing that went on then. The nursery graphs that recorded every dram of a vitamin we absorbed, and every millimeter of growth, did help to tell parents, in every country where newspapers were read, something valuable and useful about bringing up a baby. Because of the oceans of publicity we received, it was easier, for instance, to persuade mothers that children should be given diphtheria shots; we had each had three injections at intervals of three weeks when we were eighteen months old. The news that we had been vaccinated against smallpox during the third year may have led to other children being protected in the same way. (We had the vaccinations in our thighs, but Cécile somehow rubbed her wrist against the spot and so gave herself a second dosing.)

Around Corbeil, where children were usually brought up along the same lines as their grandparents and great-grandparents before them, intestinal troubles among new-born babies suddenly showed a noticeable decline. It was accepted that Dr. Dafoe's widely proclaimed insistence on hygiene was responsible for that. We were given credit for being able to give the cause of child welfare what the doctor called "the best boost in our times." Perhaps it is permissible to take pride in that. One thing we found, however, was that there was nothing to be done about catching colds. We had them every winter, and nobody could ever prevent all of us catching the infection from whichever one started to sneeze first.

The useful things that were learned make up for some of the nonsense of those times. There was the day Madame de Kiriline routed Dr. Dafoe out of his bed to join in the celebrating when the first Quintuplet tooth appeared in the gum of Annette. We were definitely late in cutting teeth, by something between three and seven months, and the newspaper reporters had kept their readers in a state of breathless suspense wondering when—or even whether?—we might have something to chew with.

Madame de Kiriline sent an orderly racing across the

road to break the news to Mom, but Mom did not come to the nursery that day. The fact of our separation from the rest of the family was already a deep wound to her feelings. Dad was usually willing and inquisitive enough to visit us, but Mom sometimes needed persuading.

One American newspaper had the sense to poke fun at all the fuss that was aroused by the eruption of a single speck of white in a baby's gum. "Germany insists on an army, navy and air force . . . Cuba tries to survive a civil war . . . the U.S. Senate, after eight weeks of tussling, passes what was then the biggest single appropriation in history, a $4,880,000,000 relief bill . . . and the major news in March (1935) on the front page is that Annette cuts her first tooth."

By now, we rejoiced in our full names. In the nursery, wearing white embroidered Madeira dresses, we had been properly christened by Father E. T. McNally, who followed Father Routhier as the parish priest. With Mom and Dad there to watch, we became Marie Edwilda Yvonne, Marie Lilianne Annette, Marie Emilda Cécile, Marie Jeanne Emilie and Reine Alma Marie.

Not long after, Dad had a falling out with Father McNally, who was a good friend of Dr. Dafoe's; doctor and priest often went on their rounds together. Dad went to the priest to complain about the doctor's severity toward one of the nurses, Cécile Lamoureux. She was, it seems, very friendly with the Dionnes, and Dad thought she was in danger of being dismissed on that account.

"What do you think I ought to do to keep her on the staff?" Dad asked the priest. The reply, according to Dad, was, "Go home and chop wood." Dad vowed never again to go to Mass in Corbeil while Father McNally remained there; thereafter he took Mom to the church in Callander.

For us to be picked up and held for the christening ceremony undoubtedly caused Madame de Kiriline some qualms. One of her strictest laws and principles was that babies should be handled as seldom as possible. "And they were never played with," she once said about us, "when it was time for them to be doing something else—to be eating for instance. That is very important."

The doctor believed in a gentler code so far as we were concerned. He came to call on us every day, by choice rather than by necessity more often than not. "I know of no greater treat in the world," he said, "than the one I receive when I enter the Quintuplets' nursery every morning and see such a rare collection of smiling, healthy babies."

As soon as we could toddle, we would scurry toward him, to cling to his legs or climb up onto his lap. He lives on in memory, in a shabby old suit that seemed never to be pressed, in a coonskin coat and otter cap in winter, puffing his pipe contentedly as he regarded his brood. We had no kisses from him, though. He was against our being kissed by anyone, particularly on the face. He looked with grave suspicion on every stranger as a potential carrier of germs, and his rule was probably a wise one. Without it, to judge by the look on some visitors' faces, we should have run the risk of being kissed to suffocation point.

He may unconsciously have come to regard us as something akin to his own children, as his own special charges to be shielded against the whole race of curiosity-seeking, nonmedical well-wishers. Much of the animosity that developed between him and Dad can be explained only in these terms. Yet the doctor realized as well as any man can how important mother love is in making a baby bloom and grow up in the security of happiness. In a guidebook for mothers that he once wrote—Cécile keeps a copy on a bookshelf—a revealing line occurs. "There are many occasions," it says, "when with lips and hands and cuddling arms, a woman can convey her love."

We knew that there was one visitor, who came across the road to see us, whom the nurses taught us to call *Maman.* But it was not possible for her to be always at our side, mothering us in the true meaning of the word, so how could we miss her on the days she did not arrive, or feel any appreciable sense of loss? The nurses—most of them, the loving ones especially—represented a kind of composite mother to us. They were always there if we had need of them, to open their arms to us, to join in the laughter and dry the tears. Whenever one of them left us for another job, we could not help weeping, because we loved them all. The most special, of course, was Yvonne Leroux, slender and blue-eyed and gay. There is a permanent place reserved for her in our hearts.

We were like the young of all living things, human beings or mammals or birds. The young cling avidly to the first warmth and tenderness that any grown-up female provides for them. Kittens, calves, colts, ducklings —in the most impressionable stages of life, we attach ourselves swiftly and unthinkingly as they do. It is an instinctive reaction, dependent on little but the need of the young for food and a haven from dangers they are too immature to face. But Mom could not understand why we wept when a nurse departed. It was still another cause of bewilderment and pain for her. It made her angry, and we in turn did not understand the reason for that.

The happiest, least complicated years of our lives were spent in the nursery. That surely is not surprising to anyone. We had everything we wanted, everything within the limits of our knowledge and imaginations. In that house of fives, we were treated like princesses. We were the cause and center of all activity. Each of us owned an enormous wardrobe of clothing, with outfits for any occasion and any kind of weather. We had dolls, tricycles, building blocks, paints, soft toys, hard toys, blackboards, easels, playthings of every description at hand when we wanted them. Hundreds more poured in ceaselessly, gifts from admiring strangers or civic organizations. These presents were either stored away for another day or given to some deserving charity.

Above all else, we had each other. Here we were, a gang of little girls ideally suited to each other. We were geared to about the same speed. We were brought up in precisely the same way. There was no turn of imagination that did not find an immediate response, since the same thought had passed through a sister's head. None of us had inclinations or abilities far removed from the others. We were a club, a society, a civilization all our own.

We slept, each in a handsome cot with her name on it, with a nurse in the room to watch over us through the night. In the grounds outside, behind the inner fence, a guard made his rounds every hour. At four-thirty, the night nurse roused herself to close the windows, which were left open summer and winter while we slept, to the consternation of most of the village. In winter, she turned up the thermostat so that the nursery would be warmed up before we awoke.

At six o'clock lights gleamed in the staff house, the only other building of any size on the estate; it was something of a mystery to us, because it was out of bounds. At six-thirty, the two day nurses came hurrying down the path from the knoll where that building stood. Then the nursery blinds were raised, and we would wake up to another day, each in her pale-yellow crib which, besides its inhabitant's name, carried a scroll on the end panel that said, *"Que le bon Jésus vous garde"* (May the good Lord watch over you).

We dressed together in the big bathroom, a giggling

crowd of little girls, sitting usually on the rug on the tile floor by the big radiator that stood under the windows. During the winters, feeding boxes were fixed outside one of the nursery windows to bring the birds in close for us to see.

We had morning doses of orange juice and cod-liver oil, and then came the hairdos. The not-very-wavy Dionne hair, which grew darker as we grew older, had to be curled. The job took more and more of the day as the years slipped by. We invariably breakfasted wearing curlers. "Early to bed and early to rise" was one rule we lived by. Another, insisted upon by the doctor, was, "Leave them to it"; the nurses were told that we were to be allowed as much freedom as possible and to be restrained only if things showed signs of getting completely out of hand.

A prayer was said before breakfast, which, after the gong had sounded, was eaten in the dining room opening off the long hall across the way from the office. The room had been specially decorated for us, in white, with three enamel-covered tables, six small chairs and a buffet. Up to the age of two, we had eaten in the day nursery, perched on high chairs in a semicircle so that we could see each other at work with mug and spoon and pusher.

In early days, we had a distinctive color assigned to each of us to identify our belongings and our places, together with a picture symbol. Newspaper stories invariably got these confused and mixed up somewhere along the line. In fact, Annette's shade was red, and she had a maple leaf to mark her chair, her clothes peg, toothbrush holder and the rest, in customary nursery-school fashion. Cécile had green and a turkey; Emilie white and a tulip; Marie blue and a teddy bear; Yvonne pink and a bluebird.

One of the staff always ate with us in the sixth chair.

Grace was said after we had settled down, and then we went in turn with our dishes for a helping of each course from the serving table, with its covered containers to keep food hot. The rule here was, "If you don't finish one course, you won't be served the next." There was no limit to the number of helpings of anything we might have, provided we had finished the main course.

We could chatter as much as we liked, but after thirty minutes we were supposed to clear the table whether we had finished or not. We each had a little tray for carrying away the dishes. Then we were off for a carefully noted trip to the bathroom; the schedules of the day called this Elimination Routine. There was no end to those excursions to the bathroom. What happened there and at the table, too, was checked off unfailingly by the nursing staff on charts entitled Dining-Room Routine Record, with entries to indicate whether or not we had showed signs of Cooperation, Unfinished Servings, Refusals or, least desirable of all, plain old Inattention.

Every month a different timetable of activities was drawn up, brought up to date to match our growth physically and, one hopes, mentally. What remains in the mind now, so many years later, is the atmosphere of carefree days, almost all of them uniformly rose-tinted by memory, with occasional sharper glimpses of a person or an event leaving a more profound impression. The overwhelming memory is of a wonderful, glowing happiness given, received and shared. We were kept as busy as beavers, and we relished almost every moment of it.

After breakfast we played in the sunroom, dragging out of cupboards the dolls, balls, woolly dogs or toy drums and trumpets we wanted, on the understanding that after thirty minutes we had to put them away again. Then we had fifteen minutes to gossip with the nurses, before Dr. Dafoe drove up at nine o'clock for morning inspection.

It is difficult to recall precisely what rooms and how many of them we had at our disposal, because, looking back, it seems that our quarters were forever being changed or expanded. The room in which we napped every afternoon had originally been the playroom. At one time the bathroom walls were pushed out to enlarge these quarters, where we stood in a row to wash our hands and faces and struggled to comb our hair. One room suddenly became equipped for music, another was set aside as the isolation room, to which one of us would be temporarily banished for defying the rules too outrageously or behaving in some way that the nurses thought beyond endurance.

When we had sprouted enough teeth to warrant it, a dentist's chair and complete equipment were installed. We paid "pretend" visits to the imaginary dentist once in a while, so that we should have no fears when the time came to submit in reality to the whirring drill. None of us minded in the least having the doctor or one of the nurses inspect our teeth or, later, having a visiting dentist work on them. We had no idea that anyone was supposed to be afraid. Sitting in the little black chair was fun; it added variety to the day.

What we objected to was the exercising. We had a special exercise to do to keep our belated teeth in good condition and correct a tendency we all had to overbite. The exercise consisted of biting on a rubber mouthpiece, then tugging at it with the fingers. We had another exercise to perform for strengthening ankles and feet, too. For a few minutes every day, we had to go through a ceremonial wiggling of our feet and tracing circles in the air with our toes. We thought we looked remarkably silly, but we were all in the same boat, so we chuckled with laughter and nobody cared.

The self-help training extended to dressing ourselves for outdoors as soon as our fingers could cope with buttons and buttonholes, with five glasses of water to be swallowed before we went outside. Small wonder there were so many bathroom excursions to record!

Sometime before our third birthday, there was an era of great excitement when we could watch workmen arrive every morning inside our sanctuary to tackle the job of putting up a new building. Until this time, the big, open-air porch had been our playground. But our guardians, presumably prompted by the doctor, realized that we needed something less public now that we were becoming more and more aware of the crowds who gathered every day.

The answer was provided by the new observatory. It was made of split logs with a red roof like the rest of the buildings on the estate. It was supposedly the first structure of its kind ever to be designed in the shape of a horseshoe, with a passageway running along its three sides. The outer wall of this promenade had no windows, the inner wall contained glass windows covered by fine-mesh wire screens. Through the windows, the spectators could see our new playground, with its lawn, shade tree, box swing, jungle gym, sandbox and wading pool. Around the lawn ran a concrete strip on which we could ride our tricycles and tug our wagons. In wintertime, a slide was erected down which to slither in our toboggans.

We went each morning and afternoon to the playground to put on a show that gave us a certain pleasure. We pulled our tricycles out of the storage room at the top of one side of the horseshoe and dashed helter-skelter around the concrete track. We made endless sand pies and cakes and castles. We piled up innumerable skyscrapers of big hollow blocks that were almost as big as we were, but easy enough to carry.

Most of the time we yelled and shrieked with joy of living, and we developed a shrewd idea of what would please the crowds most. We would venture into the wading pool with shoes and socks on, certain that the visitors in the corridors would enjoy the fun.

Emilie loved to pose on the top bar of the jungle gym like a circus acrobat and teeter there, knowing that the tourists would be busy debating whether or not she would fall. One day Marie held up a toy monkey to show for the crowd to admire. Emilie, who was an extrovert in those days, whispered to her, "You'd better put that down or people will think there are six of us."

ᢈᔑ FOUR ᔑᢈ

I N THEORY, the onlookers were invisible to anyone in
the playground. The idea was that since the passageway
was dark, the wire screening would disperse the light so
that we would see nothing of the crowds who streamed
in to gaze at the show. But of course we knew very well
that we were watched every minute that we spent at play
there.

A big, painted sign requested "SILENCE PLEASE," and
the guards forbade any tapping on the windows to attract our attention or any blowing of automobile horns
on the road or in the parking areas outside. But we could
plainly hear our guests chuckle at some antic or other,
and that was a reward we looked forward to. We even
found a way of saying our thanks, by stacking up the big
blocks against the inner wall of the observatory so that
we could wave through the screening at the vague shapes
in view on the other side.

Alongside one exit from the observatory there was a
trough of pebbles, which had constantly to be refilled,
since they vanished at an amazing rate into the purses

and pockets of souvenir hunters. They were regarded by the superstitious as good-luck tokens, like rabbits' paws and four-leaf clovers, with the significant difference that they supposedly improved fertility as well as good fortune. There was a distinct drop in the level of the trough when the Hollywood actors and motion-picture crews left after one of their expeditions to see us. Seeing what an attraction the pebbles were, the souvenir stands that lined the road outside the nursery soon began selling fertility stones at fifty cents each.

There was no apparent ban on what was sold at the stands, but one ban was strictly enforced among the visitors. Cameras and the taking of photographs were absolutely forbidden. Taking pictures was the exclusive right of the *Toronto Star* and the Newspaper Enterprise Association, a United States feature service that paid $25,000 a year into the Quintuplet bank account for the privilege.

The guardians' aim was to raise money in any number of ways to pay for the expense of raising us, with something left over to put into the bank in our names. Apart from the birthday shot that Dick Railton of *The Nugget* took, every photograph for years was the work of Fred Davis, of NEA, who eventually married Nurse Leroux. It was also important to his job, of course, to see to it that noboby snapped unauthorized photographs. In this, he was doing no more than was expected of him by the very spirit of the contracts which the board of guardians signed on our behalf.

Yet it is difficult for a contract to take into account all the niceties of human feeling, no matter how conscientiously it is drawn up. "Exclusive" was a word that was interpreted in the strictest possible way. Dad once tried to take a picture of us through a window for himself. He was rebuked for his efforts, was reminded that they infringed the legal documents and was told never to attempt such a thing again.

The description that magazine and newspaper writers attached to us as babies—"human nuggets"—proved to be all too apt. There was a terrible tendency on the part of some people to think of us in terms of property and scarcely ever in human terms. We were an object of curiosity, and therefore we could be used to make money.

One quotation summed up this attitude more sharply than any other words said about us. A man close to our family—not Dad or any relative—once complained to Dr. Dafoe about the fact that the Ontario government had made us its wards. "If you find a gold mine," he said bitterly, "the government doesn't take it away from you." One small difference between us and gold mines was that we were quite normal human beings with quite normal needs for love.

Posing for photographs was as much a part of our lives as the careful brushing of teeth, which was done as a habit twice a day. There was no end to the demand for Quintuplet pictures. Newspaper readers wanted to see the pictures, which meant that the newspapers signed contracts to obtain them. The only source for pictures was NEA, which had signed contracts with the guardians. The result was that we celebrated every holiday from New Year's Day to New Year's Eve weeks in advance, so that the photographs could be sent out in good time to NEA customers.

We poked our heads through cardboard Valentine hearts, carved pumpkins for Halloween, clambered happily on the knee of a Santa Claus who looked surprisingly like Dr. Dafoe behind the whiskers. We dressed up as instructed, in hula skirts, blue jeans, sun suits, Eskimo parkas, cowboy outfits and the dozens of other costumes that were added to our wardrobe. Picture-

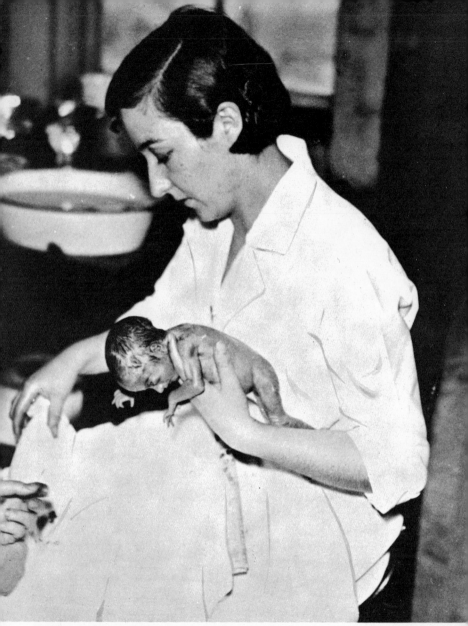

This was the beginning. Nurse Leroux had just arrived in the panic-stricken Dionne household, and our chances of survival looked a little brighter. Impossible to tell which one of us she is holding here.

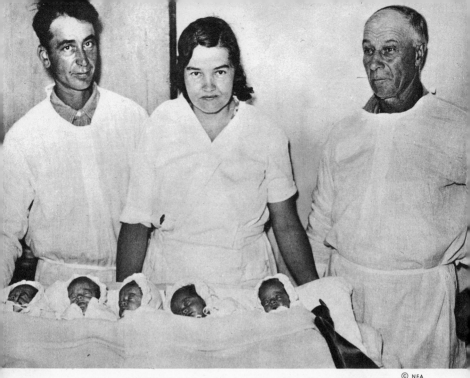

© NEA

(*Above*) The grownups, left to right, are Dad, Mom, Grandfather Dionne. The babies, according to the adults, are Marie, Emilie, Cécile, Annette, Yvonne.

(*Right, top*) The second Christmas. Santa Claus looked amazingly like Dr. Dafoe.

(*Right, bottom*) We looked forward to seeing the doctor every morning at nine o'clock. Marie is the barber, helped by Annette and Emilie. On his lap sit Yvonne and Cécile.

(*Below*) Identification by birthday cakes: May 28, 1935, one year old.

© NEA

(*Above*) Marie leads this playground parade. Sometimes we were such show-offs!

(*Below*) Here we are again with Dr. Dafoe. Everyone is feeling cheerful.

(*Above*) Our fourth birthday—and Annette, Emilie, Yvonne, Marie and Cécile are taking it quite seriously.

(*Below*) Not yet five, and in the files of the photographic agency this is already picture number 5,916! Annette, Cécile, Yvonne and Marie on top of the snow pile, Em tunneling below.

(*Above*) One of our many cousins joins us in the nursery for a pause that refreshes—surrounded by (left to right) Cécile, Annette, Yvonne, Marie and Emilie.

(*Below*) We were six years old, and the snow was fun for all five of us, though not perhaps for the shivering photographer.

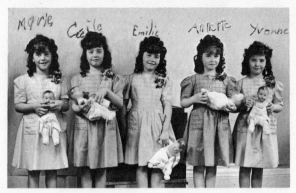

Marie Cécile Emilie Annette Yvonne

(*Above*) For the official seventh birthday picture, it was someone's idea for us to hold dolls, to show the size we had been at
birth.

(*Below*) Ground-breaking ceremonies for the Big House. The
other children in the picture are our brothers Oliva, Jr., Victor
and Daniel, and our sister Pauline.

(*Above*) A formal sitting in the Big House living room soon after we moved in: Marie, Annette, Yvonne, Cécile, Emilie.

(*Below*) Mom and Dad with half their family. We were eight and a half years old.

(*Above, left*) Our first winter at the Big House.

(*Below*) May 9, 1943, the day we each launched a Lend Lease ship at Superior, Wisconsin. (*Above, right*) Em gets ready to launch the SS *Watson Ferris*. That bottle held Niagara River water, not champagne.

(Opposite page, top left) A kiss for Claude, born when we were twelve years old.

(Top right) This picture of Mom was taken before a European vacation.

(Bottom) Mom with Claude, the youngest, and two of her grandchildren, Lise and Micheline, both of them Ernest's daughters.

A happy day for Dad. We had just been brought into the Big House. The legs belong to Annette, Yvonne, Marie, Em and Cécile.

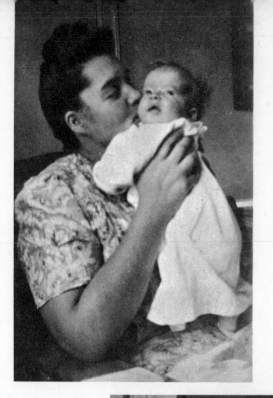

(Left) In the cathedral of Montreal. Our guide, the late Monsignor Joseph Charbonneau, Archbishop of Montreal.

(Below) The Marian Congress, Ottawa, 1947. Cécile kneels before the French Cardinal Pierre Gerbier, Archbishop of Lyon. Waiting in line are Yvonne, our sister Pauline, Marie, Annette and Emilie. The bearded priest is Cardinal Eugene Tisserant; on his left, Cardinal McGuigan, Archbishop of Toronto.

(Right) Out from the old Staff House marches our brother Ernest, with his bride, Jeannette Guindon, followed by Marie and Em, followed by Yvonne and Cécile. Annette brings up the rear.

(Below) Outside the Villa Notre Dame, 1948. In the middle of the front row sits our beloved Sister Aimée des Anges. Em stands directly behind, with Yvonne and Marie on her right, Annette and Cécile on her left.

Our one and only visit to New York, in 1950, for the Alfred E. Smith memorial fund-raising dinner. *Above,* prayers in St. Patrick's Cathedral; on the left is our music teacher, Sister Lucile des Anges. *Below, left,* Cardinal Spellman met us at the station. *Right,* at Rockefeller Center.

Now we are only four. Tea in the convent with Yvonne. Marie sits beside her, Annette on the left, Cécile on the right. Such reunions are rare, alas.

Three from the past and nine for the future! Left to right, Jean-François Allard, Marie Houle holding Monique Houle, Emilie Houle, Charles Allard, Annette Allard holding Eric Allard, Bertrand Langlois, Claude Langlois, Cécile Langlois holding Elizabeth Langlois, Patrice Langlois.

taking sessions were as good as parties. Whatever the season or occasion, we were delighted to join in.

The photographs filled whole pages of the newspapers, presumably because there was nothing quite like these baby pictures for taking readers' thoughts away from the mundane troubles that all of us are heir to. Dad did not approve at all. Fred Davis, the *Toronto Star* and NEA came close to the top of the black list, in his judgment, and that list did not grow any shorter.

Most of the experts who studied us came to the conclusion that we were a courageous lot who seldom cried or complained. Careful count was kept by the nurses of the times we showed anger or fear or other emotions. The results were incorporated in yet more charts denoting "Frequency of Emotional Episodes Per Child."

It is doubtful whether they helped the visiting expert tell who was who among us. It was better to rely on the simple rule-of-thumb which the nurses had devised. Yvonne was the biggest and Marie the smallest among us. Then Annette could be identified because she was very much like Yvonne. That left Cécile and Emilie, and if you could pick out one, the last choice was simple!

It did not always serve our purposes to be tagged so easily. One or the other of us would sometimes slip into the dining room, for instance, to shuffle the chairs around so that we could not be spotted by our individual colors or emblems of teddy bear, bluebird and so on. In any case, the seating arrangement was changed to order every week, with the thought of avoiding competition among us for a permanent place next to a favorite nurse.

Our friendly, professional inquisitors found that Yvonne once definitely showed marked symptoms of fear, and this at a nursery blind flapping on a windy night. Annette, Cécile and Marie were all scared of something or other, but it was Emilie who was the bravest in the nursery. She was the tomboy, who loved to collect pencils or chalk or butterflies and stuff them into the pockets of her smock. She was forever searching in the grass to find a four-leaf clover. One day her joy was intense because she found a sprig that had five leaves. Only Emilie had the courage needed to pose for one session of Thanksgiving pictures, when a live turkey was brought in a crate and led around on a string. She chased him with a toy hatchet in her hand, as bold as the daughter of an Indian chief.

Some of the few fears we knew were deliberately created by nurses. The unusual circumstances of our existence gave rise to all kinds of problems for them. They must have been far more conscious than we were of the crowds that besieged the nursery. Regulations were strict, and their working hours were long. They had to live more or less isolated from the community around them, and the nearest town, North Bay, was twelve miles away.

Perhaps some of them felt, in the old-fashioned way, that without instilling fear in its heart, a child is hard to discipline. Perhaps there was a desire to bring us down to earth, to treat us without the pampering we were supposed always to enjoy. Dr. Dafoe can have known nothing of what went on. Any nurse he engaged was given to understand that a good disciplinarian must not play on emotions but simply teach a child to conform to rules and regulations for the benefit of the group. At least, that is what the books say about him.

The worst official punishment for any one of us was to be isolated from her sisters. The small room set aside for this purpose lay at the end of a passageway, between the big bathroom and one of our playrooms. It was provided with a chair, a table, a few things to play with, and a pleasant enough view through its single window. This is what reporters liked to call "the jail." It was in no sense uncomfortable, but the four who were left behind when the offender had been marched off always felt that they were suffering as much as the prisoner. Punishment for one was punishment for all. We did our level best to stay out of trouble as soon as we realized what the word meant.

For one or two of the nurses isolation was not enough. Something more had to be added to bring us a sense of wrongdoing. There were nights when we slept in our cribs with our hands tied to the bars. At first this was done to curb a bad habit which we had picked up, as many small children do. But later it was done for punishment only. Mom once came in late and found us roped in for the night. She immediately pulled at the knots to untie us, then turned in a fury on the nurse responsible. That chance discovery probably put an end to the nighttime tying, but it is not possible to recall the sequence of events exactly.

Another nurse played a different trick on us, though we never could decide whether it was from malice or only from thoughtlessness. Going to the bathroom one night, we heard a scratching sound, apparently from within the walls, that scared us half to death.

"Do you hear the rats?" said the nurse, smiling sweetly, as she walked in.

We could picture the creatures running over us while we slept. We begged her to chase them away. She went out of sight, and the terrifying noise started up again. After we had trembled long enough, the scratching stopped. It was a while before we found out that the "rats" had been nothing more than her fingernails scraping up and down the wall outside.

Sometimes the Sandman came to haunt us. This was not the docile little man who, as some mothers like to explain, steals into a bedroom each evening as darkness falls to sprinkle the magic grains into a child's eyes to bring peaceful sleep and sweet dreams. Our nursery

Sandman was a monster who bellowed outside our door and threatened us with disaster unless we behaved ourselves. Again we did not solve the mystery for months and months. The voice, of course, was that of a guard invited in, against all regulations, by a nurse who wanted to intimidate us.

These were exceedingly rare events, however, that did no more than temporarily ripple the ordinary calm of our existence. Almost without exception, we trusted everyone, family, friend or stranger, equally. Whatever fleeting fears were fostered did not leave any permanent mark. The charts testified to that. Up to the age of three years and two months, the "Frequency of Emotional Episodes Per Child" showed we had accumulated only 133 "fears" among us.

Most of these were typical children's upsets. Annette saw an assortment of old hats in the playroom and something about their appearance frightened her. Cécile tried to gulp down too large a piece of orange. Marie let her wagon slip out of her hands and it went bumping down the steps. Yvonne's eggshell startled her by breaking in her hand. The only one who showed no frights like this was Emilie, the most controlled and, in a sense, at that time the most grown-up of us.

Occasionally, we had nightmares and cried out, frightened in sleep. Cécile and Yvonne had the greatest experience of these. At four o'clock one morning, the duty nurse saw a pale figure climb out of her crib and cross the room to soothe the two of them as they tossed restlessly in some bad dream. It was Emilie.

As a little girl, before illness set in and her nature seemed to turn in on itself, she was the most magnanimous of us, too, the one quickest to show kindness and understanding. The story used to be told how she fed Old Mother Hubbard's dog, who had to go hungry because the cupboard was bare. A nurse read the nursery rhyme aloud one evening before bedtime, and Emilie was deeply impressed. At breakfast the next morning, she carried a rasher of bacon from her plate over to the nursery-rhyme book, which lay open from the previous night. She carefully broke the strip of bacon in two, half for herself, and half to place on the picture of the poor hungry dog.

That impressed the rest of us more than the nurse's reading had done. The following breakfasttime, five bits of bacon were donated to the dog's picture. The nurses concluded that it was time to put a stop to this generosity, which was upsetting the dining-room routine.

"It's only a picture of a dog," one of them explained to us, "not a real dog at all. He doesn't eat bacon. He eats paper." We could recognize a hint when we heard one. On the third morning, we had five scraps of paper ready to place on the picture book.

More often than not, we fell asleep like lambs after a full day of fresh air and romping indoors and out. We were bathed just before supper, which arrived on the table at exactly six o'clock. We were encouraged always to hang up our clothes neatly and put away our shoes, each in her own cupboard. Then we climbed into pajamas or nightdresses, slippers and dressing gowns. While we waited for the chimes to announce suppertime, we would listen to the record player, which had been bought as a second-birthday present for us. It filled hundreds and hundreds of pleasant hours.

After the dishes had been cleared away, we moved on into what was known as the "quiet playroom." Here there were holy pictures hung and a statue of Saint Theresa as well as three-dimensional models of Snow White and the Seven Dwarfs. With a nurse, we knelt and recited our evening prayers with Rosaries in our fingers—the first prayer we learned was "Petit Jésus, Bonsoir."

We nodded off to sleep to soft music from the record player. They never mentioned the titles of the songs they played. We had grown quite a few years older before we recognized the fond, familiar music in arias from *La Bohème* and *Carmen* and *I Pagliacci*. That music has not lost its power to evoke those happy days, so distant now in time and place. To hear it again brings a certain gladness, and we are likely to turn to each other and say, "Do you remember?"

We had little contact with any other way of living beyond our own, the snug, secluded one inside the tall fences. Dad was a regular visitor, but from one month to another we might not see anyone else from the family. The guardians sometimes stopped by. Grandfather Dionne was on the board soon after it was set up. Then there was William Alderson, the Red Cross supervisor; Kenneth Morrison, who ran a general store in Callander; and old Judge J. A. Valin, the stately French Canadian from North Bay, who was especially welcome when he brought along his little pet monkey with its collar and chain. Apparently he did not always come to see *us*; later on, he married one of the nurses, Beatrice Provencher. Dr. Dafoe was also on the guardianship board.

On our first birthday, the guardians had reason to congratulate themselves, at least on the management of financial affairs. The bank account stood at $175,000, on the word of David Croll, the lawyer with the black mustache who served as Minister of Welfare, Labor and Municipal Affairs in Prime Minister Mitchell Hepburn's government in Toronto. Who could tell whether they regarded us as items of welfare or as a combined municipal affair?

Mr. Croll had personally written the Act that was passed into law two months before our first birthday making us wards of the Crown, not for two years as was originally planned, but until we reached eighteen. It also replaced the temporary guardians with a permanent board, made up of Judge Valin, Mr. Croll, Dr. Dafoe, and Dad, who replaced his father. But Dad often stayed away from the monthly meetings on the ground that, whatever he said, he would automatically be overruled.

The guardians had full control of all business questions. It was they who made the contracts, paid the expenses and decided every last detail of our welfare. Every contract needed the unqualified approval of the doctor, who alone could decide whether it might have an adverse effect on our well-being. All kinds of money was swelling the Quintuplet fund, which the guardians supervised, investing the capital in government securities.

The first advertisement in Dad's files appeared in the newspapers four days before our first Christmas. On behalf of the St. Lawrence Starch Company, of Port Credit, Ontario, it announced that Bee Hive Golden Syrup had been used in the formula whipped up in the farmhouse kitchen.

In 1935, there was much, much more advertising. "This morning the Dionne Quints had Quaker Oats," said one advertisement. Another reported that we were gaining weight on Libby's new homogenized food. A third urged newspaper readers to hear the very latest bulletins about us "direct from Canada TONIGHT 10 P.M. Carnation Contented Hour."

The government literally monopolized us. An Order in Council of the Dominion Government, the federal body in Ottawa, prohibited the use of the words Quins, Quints or Quintuplets in any advertisement without the guardians' permission in advance.

In 1935, too, we made our bow in a movie, and Twentieth Century–Fox contributed $50,000 for our services to the bank account. We were required to do no more than spend thirty carefully timed minutes before the cameras each day, gurgling at each other and trying to spoon por-

71

ridge into our mouths. Darryl F. Zanuck flew ceremoniously to North Bay to start production on the story, which was entitled *The Country Doctor*, meaning Dr. Dafoe. The part was originally meant for Will Rogers, but he was killed in a plane crash, and the producers had to change their plans.

Finally it was Jean Hersholt who played the role. In the kind of phrase that was apparently considered necessary to the theme, he called it "the greatest role any actor has ever been given to play." We came to know him a little in subsequent movies we made with him, in which he was always the genial doctor. He had a broad, kindly smile. We enjoyed his company. The guardians had chosen Twentieth Century–Fox over several other producers and studios with ambitions to sign us up. According to the records, Mary Pickford also had the thought of putting us on the screen.

The real country doctor insisted that his regulations be obeyed as rigidly as possible while the movie was being made. The actors and camera crew had to submit to having their throats and noses sprayed with a germicide before they were allowed into the nursery. Actors and actresses were permitted to wear whatever costumes the script called for in our presence, but those clothes had to be put in the sterilizer first and steamed to a state of asepsis. Everyone working behind the cameras wore surgical gown and mask.

It all made an astounding publicity story. The boastful announcements said that *The Country Doctor* was going to be "the greatest money-maker ever to come out of Hollywood." It did, in fact, turn out to be the most popular movie of 1936—but not with Dad.

He was invited, along with Mom, to see it at Radio City Music Hall in New York and spend a week's sightseeing there, with reservations at the Waldorf-Astoria. He hated what he saw depicted on the screen and the roars of laughter that broke out among the audience, though they had no idea that he was sitting among them. He was made out to be an amiable country bumpkin who had to climb trees to catch a glimpse of his daughters. His resentment was natural enough over this blow to his pride, and he has not forgotten it. He has said never a word to us about *The Country Doctor*, which was only the fourth picture Mom had ever seen. Nor has he mentioned any of the other movies we appeared in.

He did accept an invitation to take her to a North Bay preview of the next one, *Reunion*. An enormously enlarged picture of the Quintuplets covered the entrance doors of the Capitol Theater on Main Street, leaving only the handles showing. The girl ushers and the ticket seller were dressed up as Red Cross nurses. "All guest tickets suspended for this attraction," said the ads in *The Nugget*.

Dad could not have cared much for *Reunion* either. His good friends on the newspaper reported that the picture had been "blacklisted by the Legion of Decency and barred to children in Chicago." *The Nugget*'s reviewer found that "footage alloted the babies left much to be desired."

Mom and Dad had already tried their luck in the entertainment business and run into more unhappiness. They were tempted into it by the promoters who swarmed around like horseflies. This time another man from Chicago, Max Halperin, wanted them for what he described as a "good-will tour." This meant ten days of appearances in vaudeville theaters in his own city, in Detroit and in South Bend, Indiana.

Before they set out, Dad insisted on having the full fee deposited in his name in his North Bay bank. With this done, they left the other children in the care of relatives and took the train to Chicago. Dad had two "man-

73

agers" go along with him—Uncle Leon, who had broken the news of our birth, and Leo Kervin, who rented out houseboats. Madame Joseph Rochon, a neighbor who was also a cousin of Dad's, went along, too.

"There will be absolutely nothing commercial about it," the promoter had promised. But outside the Chicago theater where they started their tour a huge sign said, "SENSATIONAL—ONE WEEK ONLY—THE DIONNES." Whatever the audiences imagined they would see—five babies, their parents or the whole family—they nevertheless turned up by the hundreds to buy tickets.

Judged by any standards, it was an innocent and simple enough performance that the audiences paid to see. The show opened with a brief movie of the Quintuplets projected on a screen lowered over the stage. Then the orchestra in the pit struck up a tune called "Baby Your Mother Like She Babies You," while a master of ceremonies recited the story of what happened in Corbeil on May 28, which was now nine months past. He concluded by introducing first Madame Rochon and then Dad, who came out from behind the curtains in a new blue suit, and Mom in a new brown dress.

Dad made a little speech. "Mrs. Dionne and myself are glad to have the opportunity to thank you people of the United States for all the kindly interest shown us and our babies." Mom could scarcely hide her trembling. She said, *"Merci beaucoup. Que Dieu vous bénisse"* (God bless you). That was all there was to it. The spectators' curiosity was satisfied, and the next act on the program was ready in the wings.

The matter could have ended there, but Dad and the newspapers had another difference of opinion. They made much of the fact that the journey to Chicago was the first train ride Mom had taken in years. They reported joyfully, because it fitted their usual portrait of him as an ignorant peasant, that Dad and his party had been delayed at the United States border until someone scraped up the eight dollars for head tax that was levied at the rate of two dollars apiece in those days. The papers carried stories about Mom being handed the keys to the city and calling at the Lying-In Hospital, which had sent breast milk by plane to Corbeil for us, but they also printed pictures of Mom and Dad in a night club, Mom looking grim and Dad showing a certain twinkle in his eye. Neither of them liked that.

But worst of all, the reporters interviewed Max Halperin, who had some cutting things to say. He complained bitterly about the cost of the clothes his protégés had bought at his expense and the meals they ordered in their rooms, the Presidential Suite overlooking Lake Michigan, at the Congress Hotel. Dad "won't even buy cigarettes," the promoter grumbled. "He keeps me out of them all the time with his borrowing."

So another senseless storm in a teacup was in the making. Because of what appeared in the newspapers, Dad was blamed for letting publicity go to his head and for putting on an "undignified exhibition" in the United States, to the discredit of his country. Prime Minister Hepburn said cruel things about the tour and about Mom and Dad: "They have no value except as parents of the Quintuplets." Nobody ever hurt them more than that.

Dad brooded over this fresh example of what he could only interpret as the worst kind of injustice. Stringing cause and effect together in his mind, he managed somehow to pin the responsibility for his humiliation on the *Toronto Star*, linking the trip to Chicago with the rankling question of rights to Quintuplet pictures.

He sat down to defend himself in a long letter to another newspaper. The *Star*, he said, "paid comparatively little for these exclusive rights and made or should have made a tremendous sum. The paper took this opportunity of striking a blow at us, hoping we might never gain control and they would continue to make a fortune." Would the Chicago visit have been undignified, he asked, if the newspaper had not "concocted" stories about "the borrowed cigarettes, the gluttonous meals, the make-up, etc., etc., none of which ever took place?"

After all expenses had been counted and the managers had received their shares, Dad finished the vaudeville tour with something close to two thousand dollars. That was certainly better than the seventy-five dollars a week which, he was quick to point out to reporters, was what he received through the board of guardians. But it did not begin to compare with the money that was accumulating in the Quintuplet account, which he could not touch, from the contracts for motion pictures and photographs and endorsements of nursery products.

With five children to support, Dad felt that he had the right, and the privilege, to lay hold of more money than he had made so far.

⌁ FIVE ⌁

INSTEAD of the "No Admittance" warning he had angrily nailed to a tree by the front porch to keep reporters and sightseers away, Dad hung a different sign on the front of the farmhouse. "Friends," it said, "we offer for sale a beautiful, six-colored, framed picture of our Quintuplet babies. These pictures are boxed for safe carrying and each one is autographed by Mrs. Dionne and myself. Oliva Dionne. Price $1.50." It made a poignant contrast with the figures that government officials proudly quoted to show just how much the Quintuplets were worth in their own right and as an investment for Ontario.

The movie studio stepped up the fee for *Reunion* to $250,000, where *The Country Doctor* had brought $50,000. The quarter-million was also to cover two later pictures we appeared in. The guardians signed contracts for a million Brown and Bigelow calendars, which came out in fresh editions year after year. Factories were turning out Quintuplet dishes, diapers, candy, jewelry, purses and spoons. Money rolled in from the Corn Products Refining Company, the Alexander Doll Company, the

77

United Drug Company, Tiny Town Togs, Lever Brothers, the Palmolive Company, the Quaker Oats Company and Libby, McNeill & Libby, and the list is not complete. By somebody's oversight, we were not permitted to endorse the brand of rum that Dr. Dafoe had prescribed for our first formula in our farmhouse days.

It looked as though everyone was thriving and prospering except Dad. He claimed that in the first seven months after we were handed over to the guardians' control, all he received in actual cash was $111, and of that modest sum, $100 came from a newsreel company.

"Money?" he was fond of saying. "I hardly know what it is. I have never had any."

He used to quote an interview he had with David Croll before the vaudeville tour to Chicago and elsewhere. According to Dad, the Minister told him, "God never meant you to have money. Forget about your babies. Go back to your farm, and at the end of eighteen years, we'll have a million dollars for you."

Visitors to our part of the world noticed some changes, for which the money that the tourists were bringing was responsible. They spent $51 million in Ontario in 1934, in the calculations of the government. Two years later, the figure had been almost doubled, in spite of the continuing Depression, which showed no signs of lifting. The authorities in Ottawa considered that the Quintuplets were the attraction that had brought in at least one fifth of all the tourist spending. In other words, we were a twenty-million-dollar commercial property.

No matter how hard the times were elsewhere, business in Callander was booming. Taxes had been paid up and the relief rolls had been cleared. Now only the very old or the sick remained without jobs of some description, catering to visitors in the souvenir stands, the gas stations, the tourist cabins that sprang up by the hundreds along the once deserted highway between Callander and North Bay. A new railroad station was built to accommodate the people who were intimidated by the long drive north, and the transcontinental express stopped there as a matter of course on every run.

North Bay too was an oasis of prosperity. There, land that was worth $200 in 1933 could now be sold at $5,000 a lot. The hotels were filled, and on the side streets many of the private houses advertised rooms for guests in "Quintland." The stores on Main Street, selling the typical selection of hardware, sporting goods, shoes and dresses to be found in any rural town in North America, were crowded, but the equally typical finance companies and pawnbrokers found that their business had fallen away. The streets were busy with traffic, and parked cars from all over North America crowded the curbs.

"Ask any merchant, businessman or bank manager to explain the reason," said one American at the scene, "and nine times out of ten he will do so with a single word—the Quintuplets."

It was undoubtedly fortunate that our earnings were continually permitted to grow, since the cost of maintaining us went up by leaps and bounds. The nursery, the observatory, the staff house and the acreage, originally Dad's, on which they stood—everything had been charged and paid for; the property was valued now at $60,000. We paid our own living expenses, which amounted to about $1,800 a month. Most of that sum was spent on wages and buying groceries and household items in Callander and North Bay. By the time we reached the age of four, there were fourteen people on the payroll. The guardians served without salary, but Dr. Dafoe was paid a steady two hundred dollars a month as physician, and he had a secretary. The board also had a paid general business manager and a secretary-treasurer in William Flannery, a North Bay attorney. Closer to home, there were two nurses, three policemen, two

79

maids, a teacher, a housekeeper and a cook. They were all debit items in the ledgers, together with all expenses.

The doctor noted that "the children are doing much already to maintain their local community." David Croll forecast at least a dozen golden years ahead for local businessmen. "As long as you have the Quints for an attraction," he declared, "you will hear the name North Bay, North Bay, North Bay throughout the continent."

That did not exactly fit in with another, less flamboyant remark of his, made when the total assets of the Quintuplet enterprise had comfortably passed the half-million mark and income was coming in at the rate of $200,000 a year. Then he said, "The ballyhoo days are over. Now they are growing up. They are beginning to notice their surroundings, to take notice of things and understand them." We were thirty-three months old.

For most of our lives, we imagined that we had lived only through the generosity of other people, and we were taught to feel grateful. The feeling is a good one, for all of us on earth have cause for gratitude in many ways. But the financial facts of life were withheld from us too long. Discovering the truth was disillusioning, until the shock began to wear off. It was a little like a servant girl finding out that she really owns the house.

"It's a wonder to me," said Cécile then, "that we weren't charged for the milk they flew in from the maternity wards for us or for the air we breathed."

Manufacturers who received the guardians' permission to use the name "Quintuplet" or its variants, all protected by being registered as trade-marks, had to pay for the privilege in the form of royalties on the goods they sold. The ledgers of the guardianship board showed that lawyers were hired to protect these precious copyrights. We were spoken of as though we were a big business corporation, and the thought feels as icy as the winter's wind when one reads the words as a grownup.

80

"Capitalized at four per cent," said one account, "these Quint-inspired revenues make the Dionne girls a $500,000,000 asset to Ontario." There were so many people desperately anxious to cash in on us. The lawsuits that came as a result began to appear on the court calendars with the first swallows of formula that we took from an eyedropper.

The moment that the newspapers proclaimed the fact that corn syrup had been included in the mixture, the president of the St. Lawrence Starch Company gave orders for a case of their own Bee Hive brand to be shipped out to the farmhouse, along with a check that was added for good will. When the company's advertisements appeared, pointing to us as customers for Bee Hive, that brand very soon replaced a rival make as the first Canadian favorite in the shops. The company which had been ousted from favor sued the makers of Bee Hive for $150,000 in damages, claiming that it was the rival brand, not Bee Hive, that had been used in Mom's kitchen.

The case dragged on through the courts for months. Finally it was the St. Lawrence company that won the day. Nurse Leroux was the key witness, and her evidence was unshakable. She said she had a clear memory of measuring out the syrup from a can with a Bee Hive label.

So the first few hours of our lives resulted in one bitterly contested legal fight, and something that happened when we were seventy-two hours old produced another. Ivan Spear, the promoter, filed a lawsuit in Chicago for one million dollars. This was the amount of damage he suffered, he claimed, when Dad repudiated the contract that would have put us on exhibition at the World's Fair.

The announcement was made at the same time that Mom and Dad were off on their short-lived vaudeville tour. It explained why, in Chicago, Dad flatly refused to sign as much as an autograph album. He had been strongly advised against putting his signature to anything again without carefully considering it beforehand.

Mr. Spear sued everybody and anybody even remotely involved with his ill-fated plans to exhibit us, from Dad to Father Routhier, from Dr. Dafoe to Grandfather Dionne. Prime Minister Hepburn thought the whole turn of events was "disgusting and nauseating" and promised that fresh laws would be passed, if needed, to put a stop to the exploitation of the "Canadian woods babies." Dr. Dafoe took the lawsuit as a joke that could not possibly be true. Nobody appears to have been particularly concerned. In any event, nothing came of the action, which was thrown out of court.

As ever, we were blissfully ignorant of anything that happened outside the barriers that had been erected around us. At about this time, we had been given our first piano in the nursery, and we were busy learning simple French and French-Canadian folk songs: "Frère Jacques," "Maman, Les Petits Bateaux," "Sur le Pont d'Avignon," and similar tunes. The kindly inquisitors who forever kept an eye on us said that even though we couldn't learn the words, we were "surprisingly adept" at carrying the melodies.

Within a few days of returning home from the Chicago tour, Dad hired a lawyer of his own, Paul Martin, of Windsor, Ontario. Perhaps he felt it was the safest thing to do, now that lawsuits were springing up everywhere. Through the attorney, he petitioned the government to put an end to the guardianship arrangement and release enough money from the Quintuplet bank account to support the rest of his family.

One of Dad's relatives joined in the campaign in a different fashion, anonymously. In its correspondence columns, The Nugget printed, without comment, a letter signed "One of the Dionnes." It said, "If the dog at the Dafoe Hospital can be fed canned milk, cannot a bottle of cod-liver oil be found for the other Dionne children?"

It was a question that was never answered, for how could it be? Dad's petition brought no immediate answer, either. But these were straws in the wind that hinted at the rancor that was growing like some dreadful weed in so many hearts.

Dad was determined to have us and the Quintuplet funds in his own, exclusive custody. It was a kind of commitment, or dedication, on his part. Anything short of this could be only a compromise. He would accept the compromise temporarily, as a matter of necessity, while he dreamed up some fresh strategy to win from the guardians and the government new concessions which would take him closer to his ultimate goal. The idea of bringing us back under his roof and his control became an obsession. It had to be achieved at all cost.

In the beginning, poor in the material things of life, he needed the money for the sake of our brothers and sisters. But later on, his fortunes were greatly improved. The souvenir pavilion, which he opened with a partner, brought in $40,000 a year. It made no difference whatever. By then it had become a matter of self-esteem that he should win. We were such a prize. He could not bear the thought that it was the doctor, not himself, who received most of the credit for our upbringing, that our lives were governed by nurses and "principles," not by our parents.

There were very few weapons he would not resort to in his determination to win the fight. Religion was introduced into the fray. So were politics. He turned to Pope Pius XI for assistance. In a letter addressed to Rome, he wrote, "You can understand the natural sentiments of a father, a mother. We want to have our children, and above all we want them to grow up under Catholic influence." That was being done already, of course, for from our earliest days we had received instruction, which continued without interruption. The Holy Father's response to the letter was to send his benediction, which Dad had framed and hung in the living room of the farmhouse.

Making no headway in his direct appeal to the Church, he looked next for help from a totally different quarter. Edward VIII had just become King of Great Britain on the death of his father, George V, but had not yet been crowned. So a petition was sent to London, over Mom's signature. "As the date of your coronation is drawing nearer," it said, "I simply beg of you to restore to me my five little babies as a 'coronation gift.' Can't Your Majesty understand how I feel without them? Somehow I think you can, for you have an understanding nature, and I know you will extend to me your sympathy and see that my babies are restored to their parents."

She was sent only a formal acknowledgment by way of reply, stating that the "communication" was being referred to the Secretary of State. Nothing was heard of the petition again.

According to what family friends have reported, Mom had a mind to press another appeal to the king and queen who succeeded Edward when he abdicated. The opportunity came when we were to be presented to King George VI and Queen Elizabeth in Toronto, six days before our fifth birthday. It was the first time we had been allowed through the gates of the hospital from the time we had been driven in, when we were four months old.

We had been rehearsing curtsies for weeks. We had been struggling to remember that we had to call the Queen "Your Majesty," and we had been studying our so-called speeches, which in fact consisted of little more than telling her our names. Never had we known such excitement. As usual, Dr. Dafoe, with the nurses' thoughts on the subject to guide him, had ordered everything we were going to wear for the occasion. The actual details were withheld until he could make the announcement at one of his press conferences. Until that time, Mom had not been told about the powder-blue dresses we would wear for traveling, or the long white organdie with old-fashioned poke bonnets and lace mittens we would put on for the presentation itself.

Nobody on our side of the fence knew anything about the letter written on Mom's behalf, which she carried in her purse. "Is it permitted for a mother who is very unhappy to solicit your kindly intervention to the end that her family be united? You are a mother and consequently in a position to realize the sadness that wrings our hearts when we are separated from our five little girls." It went on for two or three hundred words more. Then it asked, "Let your mother's heart heed my plea and the date of May 22, 1939, will be doubly glorious and unforgettable . . ."

Mom and Dad and all the children except the baby, Victor, who was only thirteen months old, were included in the invitation to meet the King and Queen. "Our trip to Toronto will save me a trip to England," Dad said rather grandly at the souvenir shop the day before they took the train down from North Bay.

They were also invited to a luncheon for the royal visitors that was to follow the presentation. Dad at first accepted, then canceled his acceptance because he felt that he had once more been insulted by Dr. Dafoe.

The whole party of us left in a special air-conditioned train. The five of us, in the care of two nurses, had never before seen crowds face to face. Now we had a much better idea of what went on behind the screens at the observatory, what those dim shapes really looked like when the camouflage was removed. They waved to us all along the route, and we waved back and threw kisses, just as if this was one more observatory show.

The audience with the King and Queen did not last very long. Dad wore a dark-gray suit and Mom a dark-blue dress. The doctor looked strangely unfamiliar in a morning coat and a tall silk hat. King George was rather intimidating, dressed in admiral's uniform, but Queen Elizabeth looked much more reassuring in a dress of powder blue. We met under the crystal chandeliers of the drawing room of the Lieutenant General's quarters in the Parliament Building. We made our curtsies, spoke our names and handed bouquets to the Queen, whose arms were already filled with flowers.

As presents from her two daughters, Princess Elizabeth and Princess Margaret, she gave each of us a blue reefer coat. We also received a beautiful gilded model of the Coronation Coach, which we were to share. We can remember that coach better than the coats. It was a toy to gladden any child.

The newspaper accounts said that Emilie wanted to stand on her head instead of making a curtsy, but that may have been a reporter's invention. We have no memory of any such plan. Yvonne took hold of King George's hand, and Marie gave him her bouquet, which had to be retrieved so that she could present it to the Queen. Cécile decided to kiss Queen Elizabeth, so we all followed suit. The Queen stooped down to kiss each of us in turn. The reporters appreciated that. The nurses had simplified the problem of telling which of us was which in our identical dresses by giving each of us flowers of a different color to wear in our hair—Marie's blue, Annette's red, Cécile's green, Yvonne's pink and Emilie's white.

Mom exchanged a few, shy words with the Queen, but never did find the opportunity—or perhaps the courage—to hand her the carefully prepared letter. Dad, quite at ease in his business suit, spoke briefly with the King without mentioning the next shot that he intended to fire in his duel with Dr. Dafoe. His attorneys had already filed the action in North Bay courthouse. At ten o'clock the following morning, just after the air-conditioned "Quintland Special" rolled us back to North Bay station, the doctor was served with a writ for libel.

This was the new bone of contention that had led Dad to stay away from the royal luncheon. On a trip to New York earlier in the year, the doctor had been initiated as "Doctor of Litters" into the Circus Saints and Sinners, a luncheon club devoted to the lampooning of celebrities. Possibly the celebrations were not always in the best of taste, but they were seemingly always conducted in good fun. He made his appearance on the stage in front of the guests, wearing a surgical gown, with a mortarboard on his gray head and carrying a medical bag labeled "A. R. Dafoe—Mass Deliveries." As soon as the news of this event was printed, Dad was advised to sue. He could scarcely have needed much urging.

Again he looked for outside help, this time from the French-Canadian Association of Education in Ontario. This was a nationalist group dedicated to promoting and expanding the interests of French Canada. Nationalism among the French Canadians has always been a powerful factor in our country's development, though in the days we are writing of it was not the mighty force it has become today, nor had the extremists appeared to plant bombs in Montreal and paint their slogans all over the city, "Quebec Libre."

But antipathy between the two segments of our country goes back to the seventeenth-century days of Jacques Cartier, whose ships coasted along the shores of Labrador and found what he described as "the land allotted of God to Cain." Some of the wrangling over the destinies of the five of us is probably explicable in terms of nationalistic rivalries. Aggravating the feeling within our family was the question of whether we were to be brought up as English or French Canadians.

Through his new allies in the French-Canadian Association, Dad contacted an attorney, Henri Saint-Jacques, who was one of its members. He set to work with a vengeance. The suit against Dr. Dafoe was only one shot fired in the barrage, which was one more battle in the war. Writs, resolutions in Parliament and investigations filled the air with the smoke of conflict. Even in the nursery we could feel the repercussions now.

We had been brought up to speak both French and English, as most people living around North Bay were. Only a minority like Mom were perfectly able to understand English but not at all proficient in speaking it. To the dismay of many French Canadians, Ontario highway signs and shop windows do not employ both languages, French and English, as they do without fail in the Province of Quebec. Dad always preferred English to French, and to this day he writes every letter in English. That is the language, too, most frequently used among our brothers and sisters. The idea that the Dionnes were exclusively a French-speaking family is a fantasy of the newspaper writers, but it received no discouragement from Dad.

But the only language that Dr. Dafoe was fluent in was English. It was the only tongue in which he could talk to us, apart from a smattering of everyday French made up of *Bonjour* and *Comment ça va?* and such tourist phrases. Dad, with or without the support of the nationalists, could find a dozen plausible reasons why we should be taught only French. The French-language newspapers and French-Canadian societies applauded him, over the protests of English-Canadian educators and also the motion-picture companies, who could see a problem looming when it came to any future productions. Dad won, hands down. English vanished abruptly from the nursery. We were no longer taught a word of it.

Dad and the forces behind him did not wait to press their advantage. We had been accustomed to receiving visits from a new group of teachers and testers who wanted to measure our progress as nursery school pupils, now that we were growing older. Much of this work was carried out by the University of Toronto's Institute of Child Study. But that, of course, was an English-speaking institution. Suddenly the researchers were barred from seeing us for testing any more. Their work, for whatever value it might have had, was broken off, and nothing quite like it was ever started again in the nursery. It seems that a new kind of wall was being built up around us, invisible yet every bit as restrictive as the high, steel-mesh fences. But the agitation for further changing the old, familiar ways continued.

It is plain that for a long time we were governed by compromise, a little like ping-pong balls suspended on a jet of water in a fairground's shooting gallery, neither free to fall nor able to rise any higher. We continued in a state of suspension between the forces represented by Dad and those typified by the doctor. All that we personally were aware of was the sadness caused by the departure of an English-speaking nurse, though we very soon made friends with a French-speaking newcomer.

We dabbled with water colors and we squeezed Plasticine. We cut out paper dolls and hammered away contentedly in the carpenter shop set up in the north wing of the main building. We learned, with much chewing of tongues, how to write our names and how to produce a tremendously satisfying din from the drums, tambourines, bells and xylophone that made up what was politely known as the Dionne Orchestra.

We had impromptu lessons about the moles that burrowed under the lawn and also about some baby skunks, which we took at first for kittens; so did our Great Dane watchdog, Tony, who had to sit out all day in the rain in consequence, before he could be let back into society.

A curious lack of reality flavors those years in memory. We were told nothing of the tumult outside, and we would have had no means of understanding it, no frame of reference, anyway. But the spirit of uneasy compromise that ruled our lives, the need to shield us from the facts, became reflected in a peculiar, unpleasant way. We were brought up, in short, to practice deceit and accept it as a normal part of the pattern.

Most notably there was our enrollment as Brownies soon after we had attained the required age of seven. Possibly an exception was made for us and we were admitted one year early. Three hundred Girl Scouts and other Brownies took part in the ceremony on the nursery grounds. We recited the pledge, made the two-finger salute and were ceremoniously enrolled as members in St. Mary's Pack, North Bay, together with our sister Pauline.

We looked forward to learning how to tie knots and put up tents and make fires with sticks. But our expectations of fun were soon dashed. We never were allowed out to attend any pack meetings. Nor was any other meeting held at the nursery unless some Girl Scout or Brownie pack was due to call on us. Only then we were told to put on our uniforms again, to be led out meek as lambs to shake hands and salute and pose for photographs for NEA. It was not a good way to be brought up.

We were extroverted, the experts found, docile and eager to please anybody and everybody. This was especially true when it came to pleasing Mom. We would always do what she told us to, sometimes with a reward to follow in the shape of a Life Saver apiece. Candy was unknown in the nursery. We did not taste ice cream until our fourth birthday. So we were only too happy to say or do anything if Mom promised us a taste of forbidden delight in assorted flavors. More than anything else, she desired us to say, and if possible to believe, that we longed to go home to her. The words had no significance for us, and we were pleased to oblige.

She impressed on us that it was important to say this in the presence of reporters and most particularly to priests when they came to visit us. They were invariably moved by the performance we put on. One of them, a man of unquestionable integrity, reported that he found us "lonely, terribly lonely little girls."

He quoted one of us as imploring him, "Father, will you pray for the Quints, so that very soon they may go to live with Mamma and Papa? Will you please pray?" The good man also talked with Dad, who told him, "I am their father. I love them. I would not expose them to any danger. In my house, they will be better protected than they are now."

The priest wrote an account of his visit for a religious magazine. Of ourselves, he concluded that "they can only be saved, in their minds and souls, by releasing them from the nursery and sending them back home, to Mamma and Papa." We were then seven years old. The bank account held one million dollars in trust for us. We did not have to wait too much longer before we would be returned to Dad.

Everything was slowly coming his way. If we were like ping-pong balls in a shooting gallery, then it was as if someone was gradually turning off the jet of water and we were sinking closer to the earth. Dad's persistence was overcoming every obstacle.

The doctor was being forced to yield. Even his name had been replaced on the outside wall of the nursery. Visitors no longer read a plaque that said "Dafoe Hospital." Now, in a change of era and language, it was *Pouponnière des Jumelles Dionnes*.

Henri Saint-Jacques, on Dad's behalf, filed another suit against the doctor. This time an accounting of funds was demanded—"profits," said the legal papers, "that should be turned back, in whole or in part, to the estate of his wards, the Quintuplets." Once again, money was the monster, the root of evil. So many of the people around us were unable to resist its temptation. If there had been no great sums of money involved, we could all have been so much happier, so much less complicated, Dad included.

In our hearing, he did not speak openly against the doctor. But he showed no compassion for his old opponent. His words elsewhere could leave no doubt that he rejoiced in the old physician's fall from public esteem when newspaper headlines told the story of his financial frailties. He acknowledged at a momentous meeting of the board of guardians that he had unwisely signed personal contracts with companies that had the Quintuplets under their wing.

"He had it coming to him," Dad said triumphantly. When we were small, he had promised himself, "You'll see the doctor who makes fun of us laughing on the other side of his mouth when we get back our babies."

Still the money continued to roll in, though NEA had cut off its contributions directly following our visit to meet the King and Queen. All along the route from North Bay to Toronto and back, photographers had enjoyed a field day. The monopoly on picture taking had been broken, and the president of NEA was up in arms about it.

He did not mince his words. "We told the guardians," he said, "that if the Quints were taken off the nursery premises where they would be exposed in public places, we would have to consider that the guardians were not doing all in their power to see that no pictures were taken."

So the contract was considered broken because we had a taste of the outside world. Our first excursion beyond the gates cost the bank account $25,000 a year in future fees. From our limited point of view, the trip must have been worth while. There seemed to be no doubt that we could afford the loss.

In some respects, Quintuplet income, direct or indirect, was doing a little good. Dad's souvenir pavilion was showing profits, which ended the question of hardship for the family. There was electricity in the farmhouse, though still no inside bathroom. A new car was the only visible evidence of Dad's new prosperity. The gossips of Corbeil wondered what he was doing with the rest of his money.

The Quintuplet bank account, with the guardians' assent, provided funds to take our brother Ernest and sisters Rose-Marie and Thérèse out of grade school in Corbeil and send them away to be educated, Ernest in St. Alexander's College, at Pointe à Gatineau, the two girls in the Aylmer Convent, near Ottawa.

The schooling that the rest of the family received was another victory for Dad. If the two halves of his family were not allowed to live together, at least they were going to be educated together. Every day Daniel, Pauline and five-year-old Oliva junior crossed the great divide. They walked across the road to come to classes with us. We were all taught by the same governess, Mademoiselle Gaetane Vezina. She worked under the supervision of the bilingual section of the Ontario Educational Department. There was no bilingualism for us, however. Mademoiselle Vezina was under instruction to teach us only in French.

Dad and his attorney had brought that about. They had strong French-Canadian sentiment on their side, as well as the Church itself, which was painfully distressed at what was considered to be an unnatural and prolonged severance of normal family ties. Together or separately, these forces were strong enough to create serious difficulties for the government in Toronto, which was—and is—mostly Protestant and English-speaking.

The government did not risk conflict over us. Its solution to the problem of how we were to be raised was simply to let Dad have more and more of his own way, to the disadvantage and even discredit of the doctor. The Dominion government in Ottawa had virtually nothing to say about the situation one way or the other. Officials there preferred to stay out of it and leave the handling of the problem to the Province of Ontario for fear of more trouble from the Province of Quebec.

Mom and Dad and the rest of the family were free to visit us any time they chose. Regular as clockwork, we crossed the road to see them every Sunday and eat the midday meal around the big oak table in the kitchen. It would be fitting to say that we delighted in these visits and spent the week looking forward to them. That was the impression that was created, but it was entirely untrue. The five of us sat through the meals like strangers. We felt uniformly ill at ease under the inquisitive stares of the family. We felt as if we were creatures from another life, happy only when the plates had been cleared away and the time drew near for us to hurry back through the gates to the place that was home to us, the nursery.

The farmhouse made too sharp a contrast. It was a weary old place that defied all efforts to keep it even remotely spic and span. It had witnessed too many years of poverty and hardship. The hard-worn furniture was ancient and dismal by comparison with the gleaming new equipment that we had been brought up with. The painted plank walls and warped floor boards looked bare and grim in contrast with the sunny rooms in our sanctuary across the black-top highway.

Children must be forgiven if they refuse to view life through sentimental eyes. We knew instinctively the emotions of joy and contentment that Mom and Dad wanted us to feel every time we walked through their weather-beaten front door. But no matter how hard we tried to behave as we were expected to and feel in our hearts what we were supposed to feel, it was no use. It did not work. We preferred the nursery, familiar, safe and dear as it was to us.

No public voices were being raised any longer against our being returned to Dad. A sense of inevitability seemed to be the mood in everyone. Perhaps there was a measure of relief over the prospect; the troubles of the Dionnes and the disputes between Dad and the government had filled too many columns of the newspapers for too many years. But it took Mom and her Life Savers to bring the question to a climax.

The Ontario Travel Bureau, an official organization, wanted us to go on a radio broadcast which was scheduled each week, directed toward American tourists and intended to bring them to the province where we continued to be regarded as a natural wonder like Ausable Chasm or Niagara Falls. Our appearance was to be made on Mother's Day, an anniversary which we always celebrated rather elaborately. Marie was supposed to say into the microphone, "Come up and see us this summer." Then Cécile was to add, "I hope all the mothers are happy today." Finally we would all chorus, "Goodbye, goodbye."

Dad insisted afterward that he had not been consulted about the script. The first he learned about the intended performance came, he said, from reading the Saturday newspapers the day before the show. "But if I had been consulted, I would have had no objection whatsoever to the children speaking English on the radio," he said.

People on the program drilled us in our lines all day before the show was due to go on the air. But we had held a private rehearsal of our own under Yvonne's direction before that. Mom had chosen her to be the ringleader. With a few bites of candy as our promised reward, we told the bewildered radio people, "It is not nice to speak English." There was no time left to argue with us or arrange anything else. The harassed producer was forced to allow the broadcast to proceed as planned. We simply sat tight-lipped in the studio, refusing to say a word in the tongue that Dad spoke as a matter of course every day.

The newspapers had a high old time talking about the showdown that was in the making. The government in Ontario had no idea what to do. The Minister of Education, Harry Nixon, wanted us to be given lessons in English three times a week, starting immediately. But the decision about that rested with the guardians, and they were not to be hurried over a tricky thing like this.

"All we can do is *recommend* to the guardians that the children speak in English the few sentences assigned to them," the Minister said forlornly and not ministerially at all. "If they were your own children, you could take a slipper to them. But with the Quints, we can just *recommend*."

Dad seized the opportunity to come forth with one of his sleight-of-hand statements, calculated like the waving of a magician's wand to divert attention. "If it is true," he said, "that the Quints did not wish to speak English, I assume it was because they have not perfectly mastered the language yet and have a natural shyness at trying it on strangers."

If anyone knew which way the tussle over our future was going, it was Dr. Dafoe. More and more, he had been driven into the background, an ailing man who possibly lacked the vigor to fight any longer. He missed the Mother's Day fuss because he was a patient in a Toronto hospital. He had to stay there two months for a major operation, not for treatment of the diabetes from which he suffered and for which he injected himself with insulin every day. We each sent him a get-well card which we made ourselves.

Marie drew the sun and wrote, "*Que plusieurs soleils brillent encore pour vous.*" Cécile sketched a flower and told him, "*Vos cinq petites fleurs de Corbeil vous envoient une belle caresse en attendant votre retour prochain.*" From Emilie to the hospital went a picture of a cake and "*Nous vous attendons pour goûter notre gâteau de fête.*" And Yvonne's bluebird was sent "*Que ce petit oiseau vous apporte mes souhaits d'une prompte guérison.*" He saved those cards. They were among his papers, including the complete records on the Quintuplets to date, which he left to his brother, William.

Our doctor missed our seventh birthday, too. There was another radio broadcast to celebrate that. Mom and Dad sat in the studio, where Lowell Thomas was interviewing us. We wore white-flowered blue print dresses and managed again to develop what was called "mike fright" during the English half of the program, which had been planned in both English and French. When it was over, we ran over to Mom and Dad, to be given a hug for our efforts.

From the hospital, Dr. Dafoe answered a newspaperman's question as guardedly as possible: "The story of the children's refusal to speak English on the broadcast speaks for itself."

Dad must have known that the battle was as good as over, and he had won. A letter went off to Prime Minister Hepburn setting forth the terms for putting us into Dad's care. The government was content to fall in with the proposal. We were such a prickly problem for anyone. There had been talk of hurrying legislation through Parliament to cancel Dad's two lawsuits which were still pending against the doctor. But that proved to be unnecessary. They settled out of court with a truce, agreeing never again to sue each other.

Dad could afford to be magnanimous. He had been promised a brand-new house, which he was free to plan to his own specifications, to be built out of Quintuplet funds. As soon as it was ready, we were to move in with the rest of the family, reunited under one roof at last.

In February, 1942, they took us through the drifted snow to break ground for the house, to be raised on a hill that was part of Dad's farm land. It stood a little way up the road from the nursery, which would stand in clear sight of the new front windows, so that we could always see what we had left as well as what we had come to. Two weeks after that, the doctor finally resigned as our own medical supervisor. He was defeated.

"I feel that my period of usefulness is over," he said. "I hope I have done a good job." Mr. Hepburn was more frank about it. "His position," he said, "has been made almost impossible by reason of the fact that the children are not allowed to speak English."

Allan Roy Dafoe paid a final visit to the nursery when he came out of the hospital. We posed together on that sunny May morning for one or two more pictures to add to the collection. He looked much older and very frail. It was his fifty-eighth birthday. We politely wished him health as a kind of goodbye, but we showed him none of the old warm affection, and we did not hug him as before. We were old enough to know that Mom and Dad did not want us to do that. We were anxious to please. The little doctor did not allow the hurt to show on his face or in his manner.

It must have been during that winter, waiting for the

new house to be finished, that the family left the farm-house, where living was at its lowest ebb in cold weather, and moved in with us. Upstairs rooms were cleared for them, though it was a tight squeeze to fit everybody into the *Pouponnière des Jumelles Dionnes.* The division between the two halves of the family was disappearing by this time so far as outward appearances were concerned. All the children who were home took daily lessons with us. We ate the same food cooked in the same kitchen. We were supposedly getting to know each other.

The new house supposedly, too, had all frills and fancies eliminated at Dad's request, the construction cost cut to the bone as a wartime economy. Yet it finished as one of the grandest homes in northern Ontario. There was nothing approaching its elegance for miles around. There were ten bedrooms, five bathrooms, a playroom, a music room. There was a room known as the *salon de cuir* since all the furniture in it was upholstered in leather. The dining room was big enough to seat fourteen people comfortably at the enormous table, which was kept covered in oilcloth.

The exact price of it all remains something of a mystery, but Dad has told visitors, "It cost me $75,000, not counting the furniture."

He worked with the architects on the plans for this truly imposing monument to his victory, and he hired a Parisian decorator to help with the furnishing. There was a porch with a sun deck over it, built-in mirrors in the bedroom walls, bell pulls in every bedroom, which were connected with the room where a nurse was supposed to sleep. No nurse was ever hired, but we had some fun playing with those pulls and making the bells ring. The room intended for the nurse became a guest room, painted white. Among ourselves we named it "Paradise," because this was where we sometimes hid candy and where Christmas presents were always stored in advance.

To the left of the wide front door, down the tiled hall, Dad had his own red-carpeted library, which also served as his office, with a crystal chandelier, a black-marble fireplace and rows of books lining the walls. Later, in the back yard, out of sight of the highway, he had a grotto built of uncut field stones to shelter a stone figure of the Virgin that stood four feet tall. On summer evenings, we were sometimes taken out there to kneel and say our prayers. In bad weather, we leaned out of our bedroom windows, elbows on the radiators, and faced the statue when we prayed.

A broad staircase led from downstairs to the upstairs hall. At the turn in the stairs, there was a landing, and on its windowsill Dad installed another statue of the Madonna, which someone had presented to us. We were encouraged to stoop and kiss the feet every morning first thing as we came downstairs. Then somehow one hand was broken off, and it never was repaired or replaced.

Around the whole property Dad had a steel-mesh fence erected, similar to that which had separated us from the world before. The gates were unfailingly locked every evening and opened up again in the early morning when it was time to go out and milk the cows that were kept in the barn to the rear of the house. Behind the fence, watchdogs roamed the grounds.

It was the saddest home we ever knew.

⊷§ SIX §⊷

R EUNION, which the world had been taught to believe
was all we lived for, came as an anticlimax. We
moved out of the nursery after dusk one evening, to
make our way up the hill to the Big House, which looked
even bigger in the darkness. We carried a few of the
sentimental possessions that we treasured most, bundled
under our arms. We felt not unlike bundles ourselves, as
emotionless as string and as flat as wrapping paper.
There was nothing to mark the end of an era. No party.
No ceremony. No excitement. Our family did not go in
for that kind of thing.

The fable was that we had always felt, up to this
moment, like institutional children, separated by cruel
law from the rest of the family. "*Émigrées* from our home
but never from our hearts" was what Dad had called us.
We were alleged to have hated everything about the
nursery and every minute we spent there. Mom once
brought Rose-Marie into the campaign to spread that
impression, after she had come over the highway to
visit us.

101

"I saw the little jail where they put the Quints when they are naughty," our sister told *The Nugget*. "It had a key in the lock. I wouldn't like it at all, being shut up in such a place. When I saw that dark room, I almost cried. Some day the Quints will be back with us, and then everything will be perfect."

Reunion must have shattered so many dreams on both sides of our divided family. We had no wish for it. The last thing we wanted to have to do was leave the nursery. It was a haven to us, not a prison. It was familiar and friendly, the place where we had laughed so much more often than cried; we had grown there from babyhood to childhood and had loved it as the only home we knew. We were uneasy about the unknown years ahead with the family who we sensed had mixed feelings about us. For the longest time after the reunion, we used to dream of being back where we felt we belonged. Occasionally, the dream still returns, and it is like being carried away to another planet.

We were transferred into the Big House as a conquered army might be, one group of five clinging together as if for protection against the inquisitive looks of the other six brothers and sisters. Dad had delayed moving until the place was ready down to the last ash tray, smelling of fresh paint, and with new rugs and unsullied furniture. We were put by pairs into the bedrooms that had been prepared for us. That dismayed us from the start, since we were not accustomed to being separated. Annette went in with Cécile, Yvonne with Emilie, Marie with Pauline, whom Dad liked to introduce as "the sixth Quint."

New patterns were rapidly established for us. The most important lesson, to be learned immediately now that we were all together away from outsiders' eyes, was to show beyond doubting that we truly loved our parents. Somehow it had to be proved to them that the years of turmoil and struggle had been worth the cost. Of all the tasks, this was the hardest, impossible to achieve satisfactorily, because it meant acting out a pretense.

A good-night kiss was expected from each of us for both of them—a simple enough and normal thing, it might be imagined; yet it was far from that. If by any chance we forgot and hurried up to bed, Dad would fetch us down again at Mom's insistence and have us gather around to kiss first her cheek and then his.

They tried so hard to make us feel for them in our hearts, but nobody can command love. They had forgotten, like everyone else who had been caught up in the struggle over us, that the years slip relentlessly by and all children grow older. The passage of the years turned reunion into an empty victory. What might have worked when we were younger and more readily molded into different habits had little chance of success when we were already nine. We were too old.

Come what may, we had to be taught to mix with the family, when every instinct urged us to keep to ourselves, to shy away from these brothers and sisters whom we did not know very well. But Dad said we were obedient, if nothing else. We did what we were told, though we did not always meet with encouragement. We clearly seemed as strange to the family as they did to us. Some of them seemed to go out of their way to say wounding things about us, about how they had all been happier before we came into their lives. It was a bizarre situation. We spoke French, because that was what we had been taught to do, and our English was rusty. Our brothers and sisters spoke English and made fun of our efforts to talk as they did. We envied them their skill and winced at their laughter.

Like lost sheep, we tended to herd together for comfort and consolation, but this was frowned upon by Dad, who wanted us to become part of the family in every sense of the word. He kept us separated from each other whenever he could, to instill the thought that we should regard ourselves not as five of a kind but as eleven brothers and sisters. The rule was that the others could do homework in their bedrooms. We were not allowed to. We had to sit in the living room, under Dad's eye, while we struggled through our assignments. The old newspapers contain many a story deploring the fact that the Quintuplets grew into sullen, sad-looking girls. We could not entirely disguise our feelings. They showed on our faces.

It could have done nothing else but harden Dad's heart. The masks of pretense had to be worn on many occasions, but who could tell whom we deceived? Dad wanted us to keep our appearances for the sake of prestige and family pride.

We had not been long in the Big House when Dad told us that Dr. Dafoe was dead. Only a year had passed since our farewell to him, but it seemed like eternity. He had been taken into North Bay hospital with pneumonia, but he had waited too long before the ambulance was called. Five minutes after he was put to bed, his life came to an end. Those who knew him better than we say that he never recovered from his operation. They also say that the icy goodbye he received at our hands came close to tearing his heart.

Dad broke the news of his old antagonist's passing with the customary lack of emotion showing in his expression. We heard it in the same way, feeling sorrow for the doctor who had been a daily part of long ago, but concealing the sadness, because we knew, without being told, what Dad wanted us to feel. One more important part of the past, the fun we had had with the doctor as small children, had to be hidden from view.

In the printed accounts of how we were responding to our new circumstances, to this new era in the Big House, truth and falsehood are almost inextricably blended. For our tenth birthday, we received a pony, "Belle," as a present, or so the newspapers said, to Dad's cue. We were quoted as exclaiming, "A pony—a real live pony for our very own. Papa, papa, we have wanted so much to have a pony!"

The birthday gift, it was said, was "only one of the delights of their freedom." To be more accurate, "Belle" was given to Daniel, though she had been bought from Quintuplet funds. It was by no means the last time that we found what we read in the newspapers about ourselves was not necessarily true. More often than not, we could find out in advance what we should be receiving as a gift on any occasion simply by turning to *The Nugget*, which was conscientious reading for all us Dionnes.

Dad liked to pass on the news in good time to his friend, Mort Fellman, who had succeeded Eddie Bunyan as editor. Then Mr. Fellman could count on getting some more paragraphs about the Quintuplets into the newspapers by way of the Canadian Press, Dad could be sure that the item expressed his view of things and also that his name would be mentioned favorably, which of course meant a lot to him.

Mr. Fellman was forever grateful. He used to say that there was only one secret Dad ever kept from him, and that was the story of Emilie, who showed the first signs of epilepsy not long after we left the nursery. Brought up as we were under hospital conditions, with none of the average child's exposure to ills and chills, we had very little natural immunity. In our early days in the Big House, we all came down with a succession of ailments, but nothing so grave as Emilie's.

The family considered her illness to be a shameful thing. We were warned never to mention it to outsiders. In Corbeil, there was a superstitious dread of the disorder, as though it were the black plague of the Dark

Ages. To the simple people of our neighborhood, epilepsy was something to be discussed only in whispers, and then only behind the sufferer's back.

The Dionnes were ashamed, so we kept the secret. In our ignorance, we believed it was all we could do. From what doctors know nowadays, it is not likely that she could ever have been cured of the attacks, but they say that modern care and medicines will hold the seizures in check and the epileptic can lead a perfectly normal life. Emilie had no such care.

Her first attack came one morning at about seven o'clock. Yvonne heard an involuntary cry from the other bed in the room they shared. She jumped out immediately and hurried over to see what was wrong. It was clear that something was alarmingly wrong, and she ran down the hall for the rest of us.

Our first instinct was that we should treat Emile ourselves, without seeking the family's help. We thought we could nurse her as we had looked after dolls when we played doctor and nurse, which was one of our favorite games, enjoyed many a time in the nursery. But the color of her face and the ceaseless twitch of her muscles terrified us. We realized within seconds that the situation was beyond us and that we should have to turn to Mom and Dad. There was panic all through the house that morning.

At last someone telephoned the doctor, a French Canadian who had succeeded Dr. Dafoe and had attended to the rest of the family from the time Oliva junior was born in 1936. By the time he arrived, Emilie was lying in a quiet coma, drifting gradually into sleep in the classic pattern of these attacks. Years later, that doctor was quoted as saying that he had been surprised by the disclosure that she was an epileptic, though he acknowledged there had been "much hearsay." He had

106

heard that she had attacks like fainting spells, but not of a violent nature, he said.

As she grew up, the attacks occurred more frequently, sometimes several in the course of a week. An argument within the family about us, or any stormy scene from which she could not escape, was usually followed by the telltale giddiness and then unconsciousness. When adolescence began, she had a seizure, as regular as the calendar, month by month. We learned enough to be able to treat her ourselves most of the time, slipping the handle of a spoon into her mouth to prevent the teeth clenching the tongue, watching her every moment to make sure she could not hurt herself unknowingly. The cry coming from her bedroom, then Yvonne hurrying in to wake the rest of us—this was an accustomed part of life, too.

Though we were forbidden to take ourselves off to our bedrooms and club together there, we went to bed early whenever we could. In the summer, it was possible to spend a great deal of time outdoors. In the winter, when the weather slowed the pace of living to a crawl and the older members of the family passed the hours sitting at the dining-room table with a deck of cards, we retreated between the blankets.

Dad was a different being from the gaunt, harassed individual who appeared in the early photographs. He was very much the man of affairs, able to talk knowledgeably to anyone who asked about his family and the Quintuplets. Publicity had made him an important figure in Corbeil, and he was fond of playing the role of host in his handsome house. When neighbors were asked in for an evening, we were invariably part of the show, to be ushered in for inspection. Usually we were sent to bed before the guests arrived.

That did not keep them out of our rooms, but when Dad took his visitors on the usual tour of the place, we lay quiet as mice, pretending to be fast asleep so that we would not be put on exhibition. Mom was well aware of our tricks. "I know you are not asleep," she would whisper before she closed our doors again, but she did not rout us out of our beds.

Sleep was always a blessing. Usually we were weary enough not to be tempted to spend much time in bedside gossip. We would flop down and be lost to the world almost before our heads touched the pillows. When we moved into the Big House, Mom had two daily maids who came in from the village to help with the endless cooking and cleaning for a family numbering thirteen people. But the maids did not last long. Instead, Dad put his children to labor in their place.

All eleven children had chores to do in theory, but in practice most of the duties seemed to fall on our shoulders, perhaps because we were too meek to resist and too anxious not to provoke anybody's anger with us. Dad had hired men to work in the fields for a while. We had to serve them their meals in the kitchen, bolting down our own food within the ten minutes allowed us, so that the men could eat exactly on time.

Besides having undisputed power over us, Dad had been granted control of all the money banked in the Quintuplet accounts and the properties owned in our names. Exactly what this amounted to was something we did not discover for years and years. The last member of the original board of guardians, stately old Judge Valin, resigned when he reached the age of eighty-nine, leaving Dad as the only "visible" member, in the official phrase. There was another, almost unseen supervisor in the background, Percy Wilson, an amiable man appointed by the government to watch over the finances. Dad had to follow a practice of submitting monthly accounts to him, but they got along famously, and there were no questions asked about spending. Mr. Wilson, of

Scots-English ancestry, could speak some French, and there was a twinkle in his blue eyes. Dad called him "the answer to one of our prayers."

For all the former outcry raised about the shows we put on for the public in the observatory, these were in fact continued until we were ten. Toward the end, they amounted to nothing more than an increasingly self-conscious appearance with our brother and sister school-mates in the old playground. The war, bringing the rationing of tires and gasoline, had cut attendance to a trickle in comparison with the torrent of people that had once flowed up the highway. The performances had lost all importance for us. They had become a tiresome, thankless chore, like so many others. None of us remembers the last time we were on view or the last of the curiosity seekers who came to inspect us.

At the back of his mind, Dad nursed the thought of keeping us in the public eye and somehow getting us back into movies. He used to speak frankly about it when we were babies. "Not only will there be no vaudeville stage when we recover them," he said, "but their pictures will not be in newspaper ads and on tin cans and candy boxes. What my managers and myself would do is accept a moving picture occasionally and the use of the name 'Dionne Quintuplets' for a few high-class articles."

He no longer spoke openly of any plans for our employment, but he did his best to keep the Dionne name alive by accepting invitations for us to appear at Victory Bond rallies and similar patriotic events, while he stage-managed what he possibly hoped would be the start of a career for us as entertainers.

We were constantly being taught songs and drills and dances by the nuns who were our teachers in the class-rooms in the nursery, where we continued our schooling with our brothers and sisters. Mother's Day was a bigger occasion than ever in the family now, when we would present bouquets of roses to Mom and put on little shows for her in the basement playroom of the Big House on the temporary stage that Dad set up.

He chose that setting for an eleventh-birthday concert that outdid everything to date in size and scope. The stage was dressed up with the Union Jack, Stars and Stripes, Tricolour and a "V for Victory" that was plugged into a light socket. With Daniel as master of ceremonies, and Rose-Marie, Thérèse and Pauline appearing, too, we kept going for two hours that night. Dad had invited an audience that comfortably filled the room—neighbors, priests, the doctor, the lawyer, friends, relatives and Percy Wilson.

The nuns must have spent weeks sewing the costumes, with one or two items bought in North Bay, where the Quintuplets had charge accounts at Woolworth's on Main Street and at the local branch of the T. Eaton & Company chain of department stores, which was a few steps along from Woolworth's. For most of the program, we wore ankle-length taffeta, while we sang as a chorus of five and joined our three other sisters in songs that we had rehearsed over and over again. We also had a part in what Mort Fellman described the following morning as "a lovely French minuet revealing the children's joy over the liberation of France." "Quint Concert Makes Big Hit," said the headline in The Nugget.

The grand finale was grand indeed. With the other children, we put on handsome white uniforms trimmed with red and blue, and tall guardsmen's helmets, the kind that drum majorettes prance around in. We sang victory songs and marched our legs off, recited prayers for Allied fighting men and put in some good words for the sale of Victory Bonds. Before the curtain fell, we got out the drum, triangle, xylophone and tambourine and banged away to our hearts' content.

It was a most satisfactory evening from our point of view, and Dad hinted at greater glory for the future. What actually was in store for us, he was asked. "I have some plans," he told his friends that evening, "but I am keeping them to myself for the present. You see, I might possibly change my mind."

Whatever he planned, he had Percy Wilson with him. Mr. Wilson, with a glow of enthusiasm in his eyes, made a speech to the audience. "I have always thought that the Quintuplets are here for a special purpose," he declared, "for the building up and the uniting of our country. I feel too deeply moved to speak. I am just happy about the whole thing. I wish them to continue to honor their mother, their father, their church, their language, and to be great little Canadians."

Halfway through the show, as we had carefully rehearsed beforehand, Mom was presented with an armful of roses and Dad with a single flower for his buttonhole. The main present we received for the birthday was a movie projector equipped for sound, bought from Quintuplet funds, and bicycles paid for in the same way. For some reason or other, Dad decided that it would be an extravagance for us to have a bicycle each. We had to share two among the five.

They added nothing in the way of freedom. We were allowed to ride them only around the grounds behind the fence or, by special dispensation, up and down the hill on the road outside, but then only within clear sight of the front windows of the house. Marie, with revolt stirring behind the mildest manners of any of us, once took off on her bicycle and literally went over the hill, carefree for the moment, heading for she did not know where. But Oliva junior was watching her, and he scampered off to tell Mom. That meant trouble and an end, for the time being, of Marie's adventuring over the hills and far away.

Giving and receiving presents of any description created a special set of problems. It was the rule that we must remember everyone in the family on his birthday and at Christmas, without necessarily having gifts from everyone in return. One Christmas, for instance, we were each told to draw a single name written on a slip of paper from a hat. In this fashion we would find out which brother or sister would be buying the single present we were to be given in the name of all.

In general, if anything went wrong, if any argument broke out, it was we who were most likely to be blamed, the strangers in the house. Who could ever count the times we heard, "We were better off before you were born, and we'd be better off without you now"? Who would want to remember the details of discord in any event?

Dad could only have been disappointed at the way things turned out. The hopes he had once had were shattered, along with his fervent belief that once we were back with the family everything would be well again. His smiles were reserved for the public appearances he made and for the photographers. At home, he grew into an increasingly somber soul who could not find it in himself to praise us for anything we struggled to do. The hours of pleasure that we could count on were spent in the playroom; we slipped away together there sometimes to put a record on the phonograph and dance sedately two by two—to waltzes, mostly, never to jazz. There was no television, of course, in those days, and music of any kind on the radio distracted Dad. He listened to the war news, not much else.

For one inexplicable period, the playroom was also our personal dining room. We must have broken one of the long list of rules by which our behavior was to be governed. So in consequence we were consigned downstairs while the rest of the family ate dinner. While steak was served upstairs, we ate Puffed Wheat night after night down below.

It was not entirely humiliating. Out of sight of Mom and Dad, we were spared the admonitions to "sit up straight" that marked mealtimes, with a finger poked into the small of the back to emphasize the point. We were careful, though, to obey one regulation even when we were being spared scrutiny in the playroom. We made sure that our plates were left clean to the last crumb.

Mom was a good cook, and watching her at work in the kitchen was a good way to learn. Marie was the best among us, a light hand at baking, especially with a butterscotch cake. Most of whatever happiness she knew came from Mom's praise for her skill.

Calories were something unknown to Mom. We all suffered to some degree from problems of weight. We were chunky, to say the least. She thought that fresh milk and plenty of it was the sole secret of keeping healthy. We had to drink it by the quart as long as we remained at home. Coffee was served to the others by the time they reached fourteen years old. We were not allowed to taste a cup of it until we were twenty.

Similar restrictions applied to all the clothes we wore. Either Mom made our dresses or, more often than not, bought them at Eaton's. The usual procedure was for her to go without us to North Bay and bring back a saleswoman with an assortment of clothes from the store for us to try on. That took most of the fun out of shopping. We spent whole evenings standing like dummies in the living room, putting on and taking off frocks that did not appeal to our youthful tastes in the least.

But arguing with Mom or anyone else was against the rules. We did what we were told and wore what was chosen for us. Her taste ran to big flower prints. We were short in height and chubby around the middle, and the patterns swamped us. We appeared dumpier than ever. But that was not what concerned us most. As we grew older, our brothers seemed always to be trying to peek in on us while we were undressing. That may not be unusual in many families, where elder brothers tantalize their sisters, yet we were painfully aware of the embarrassment and unable to bring ourselves to complain.

To visit North Bay was a rare adventure. Mostly we stayed in the house or within the fence or on Dad's rock-ribbed acres, as secluded as in a convent. When we did get to town, we were whisked there by car, the group of us together, in the company of brothers and sisters. Together, we were conspicuous, and the stares we encountered made us uncomfortable. We scurried along Main Street or Ferguson Street, which divides the town in half, with our eyes downcast, self-conscious to the extreme. Going into a store was an ordeal to be encompassed in the briefest possible time.

The justification for the precautions was the fear that we would be kidnaped. That was why we were not allowed to go out alone, why we were hurried through the streets and watched every minute. Much of our enforced seclusion made sense only in terms of fear.

The Lindbergh baby had been found dead after being kidnaped almost two years to the day before we were born. When we were ten months old, reports appeared in the newspapers to the effect that "daring American masterminds" had made plans to snatch us from the nursery as soon as the winter's snows had melted from the highways. The kidnapers would make their getaway by car over the United States border to Sault Ste. Marie, three hundred miles away. There a plane, waiting with its engines warmed up and ready to go, would whisk us away to destinations unknown. Their purpose, as reported with complete solemnity by reporters, was not to hold us for ransom, but to put us on exhibition, with the gangsters reaping their profits from the admission fees. It is impossible to believe that anyone took the tale seriously. Neither Dad nor Dr. Dafoe had heard a word about it, but the government was taking no chances. The guards at the nursery were warned to be on the alert.

Dad and the doctor apparently suspected each other of drumming up scares about kidnaping as a weapon in the battle of nerves over our safekeeping. One school of thought detected that this hair-raising talk of kidnapers flared up whenever it looked as if Dad might succeed in wresting us away from the guardians' care. The suspicion was raised then that we should be an open invitation to criminals the moment we left the safety of the nursery.

The other side stanchly believed that any kidnaping that might occur would be committed only in Dad's interest. According to this theory, it was the only means by which he would ever get us away from the nursery, and the flight would continue out of Ontario, so that we should be beyond the reach of the Ontario courts and the special laws concerning us.

No matter whether or not either side had a shred of evidence to support its fears, we were nevertheless guarded like crown jewels in the Big House, just as we had been before we gained what was known as our "freedom." Apart from the fence, the watchdogs and supervision by other members of the family, police patrolmen were kept on call to escort us wherever Dad wanted to take us and whenever they were asked for.

Before he took us to a movie in North Bay, Dad would often telephone for two policemen. They roared along ahead of his car and behind it as he drove us into town. The little procession, which gratified some deep-seated desire of Dad's for recognition, seemed incongruous in that rural setting. It inevitably singled us out for the attention that we dearly wished to avoid, and it never failed to dampen the pleasure of being allowed out

115

of the house. The guards were not content to leave us at the door of the theater. They watched the show from the back of the house while we sat side by side in a row in full view of the rest of the audience, embarrassed by the commotion our entrance produced.

The same fear of allowing us to mingle with the supposedly hostile and dangerous world ruled out any thought of our making friends with other children than our brothers and sisters, and they had little time to spare for us. We were discouraged from seeking each other's company, but what we could do was work. Indoors and out, there was no limit to that as a means of spending our time.

We had to scrub floors and clean bathrooms, every item of plumbing in them. We had not known such tasks in our nursery days, and it would be wrong to say that we greeted the tasks enthusiastically. We milked the cows and fed the chickens, welcoming for the most part the hours passed working outdoors because it was a joy to escape from the closer supervision we were accustomed to inside.

In the spring, we helped to shear the three or four sheep Dad kept in the field behind the house. Muscles began to develop under the fat that encased our bodies. Those muscles served well at haymaking. Working with a pitchfork, tossing bales of hay up onto a truck, is not easy. Neither is carrying bags of animal feed on your back. But we felt it to be our duty in this strange new life, and we dared not be accused of loafing.

The whole family, including Mom, held Dad in awe. It was not that he was heavy-handed in his punishments, but that we were dominated by the force of his will. If he said a job had to be done, all of us accepted the command without question. Nobody argued with Dad; to disobey was unthinkable. Yet in an almost indefinable fashion, he was afraid of Mom, as if there lingered in his

116

heart a sense of guilt or obligation for fathering the five daughters in a single birth and so producing the apparently insoluble problem of what was to be done with us.

In each other's presence, they competed to see who could treat us more strictly. There was no end to their instructions to do this or not do that. But when Dad was not in the house, we could look forward to hearing from Mom the words of praise for a job well done which we did not hear from Dad and which she refused to utter in his hearing.

Only once, so far as can be remembered, did Dad show a similar sign of curbing kindness or concealing it. When Mom was away for a matter of hours, perhaps on a shopping expedition to North Bay, he brought in a box of chocolates for us to share. It was such a rare treasure that we were undecided about what to do with it. After tasting some of the chocolates, we hid the rest under a bed so that Mom would not discover them when she returned. Before she could find out what Dad had done, we had emptied the box and thrown it away.

In her actions, Mom showed sides to her nature which she did not put into words. Annette was not her favorite, but one day when Dad took Cécile, Marie and Yvonne to Ottawa to see a dentist, Mom went out of her way to pay special attention to her. For that day, Annette caught a glimpse of the warmth hidden under Mom's everyday manner.

That affection might have warmed the feelings of us all in its glow, if only we had not been caught up in a situation beyond the ability of any of us to understand. But Mom and Dad could not see inside our hearts, and we were too young to see inside theirs.

✑ SEVEN ✑

IF LOVE BEGETS LOVE, GUILT BEGETS GUILT. The air of the Big House was thick with it. If love casts out fear, then guilt invites fear in. The natural affections that develop within a family had little chance to grow among us.

If Mom and Dad behaved toward each other as though they had been partners in some unspoken misdeed in bringing us into the world, we were drenched with a sense of having sinned from the hour of our birth. The thought was drummed into us that the discord in which the family lived much of the time was all of our doing.

"You are a family by yourselves, and we are another one," our brothers used to say.

"Mom was a slim woman before you were born," we were told. "It was you who made her put on weight."

"Dad had no worries before you came along," they said, "but you split the family in two. You spoiled everything."

We were convinced that we had brought misery and

118

nothing else upon people whom we ought to love. We were riddled with guilt in all our thinking, and we knew of nothing we might do to expiate it. We could be dutiful, obedient, hard-working, but how could that possibly erase the crime of our existence? We shared a daydream that we spoke of to nobody else but each other, and then only in our bedrooms late at night or outdoors in solitary places where we could not be overheard.

Annette, Cécile, Emilie, Marie and Yvonne all whispered it. "If only I could have been a single child." We had no other ambition to equal that unattainable desire. Saying it, we would instantly think of each other and realize the enormity of the thought.

Years after, in the clearer light that shines now that we are miles away from those scenes, it is not difficult to see what might have been done to quiet the pain of existence. If Dad had been willing, we could have been sent away to school. Thérèse and Rose-Marie had gone off as boarders. So had Ernest. Perhaps it would be decided that we could go away, too. We used to try to imagine what it would be like, to get away from the too familiar scene, to explore the ways of people who were not confined behind a fence. If the power of wishing, five at a time, a dozen times a day, had been able to move mountains, then we might have had a slim chance. But wishing did not make it so. The more we longed to be separated, with one sent to school here and another there, the more remote from reality our ambition became.

We dared not press the idea or argue the cause with Dad. He felt that he alone knew what was good for us and demanded the last word on everything. Sometimes we tried to guess what was on his mind, what he planned for us, but it was impossible.

We were treated as five who really amounted to one, five of a kind so close to each other and alike in every

119

respect that we were virtually indistinguishable. We could not possibly have separate identities or desires. That was how we had been brought up so far, and that was how it was going to continue. When Mom bought us clothes, they were five of a kind. The same for coats, hats, shoes, gloves, scarves, everything. Wearing them, we felt as though we were in uniform.

We had been ordered to mix with our brothers and sisters as if we were ordinary members of the family, but neither they nor we believed this to be true. There was a difference in us, no matter how we regretted it. We were caught, it seemed, between two fires—wanting to be treated as individuals, which was not allowed, and wanting to keep together as a group united by a special bond of sympathy and understanding, one for the others. For the sake of appearances, and for the publicity that Dad enjoyed so long as he could control it, we had no choice but to remain the Dionne Quintuplets, five adding up to one uncertain being that was expected to duplicate itself five times over in everything it did or said or thought.

Dad had once sent our hopes soaring by agreeing that we should be sent to separate schools. But when it came to the test, he found it was unthinkable to split us up into individuals. Fear that we might be kidnaped, pride of a kind in having control of us, determination that somehow we must be absorbed into the family—all these could have been factors in his decision. Anyway, instead of our going off to school, the school was brought to us.

At first, the nursery building was turned into a private educational institute reserved for the family—ourselves, Daniel and Pauline. The teachers were five nuns, Sisters of the Assumption, who were assigned to the task. They came to live in what had been the staff house from the little, strongly ecclesiastical town of Nicolet that stands on the river of the same name between Montreal and

120

Quebec. Mom and Dad did not always see eye to eye with them on the question of how or what we were to be taught. There was no lack of argument between them.

A caretaker was appointed to look after the new school premises. Leo Chalifoux was a family man, and he brought his wife and children with him to his job. To us, it was like discovering a different race of people. It brought us our first playmates and first close contact with a family other than our own. Denise, Lucille and Leo junior were like emissaries from another planet, full of the most intriguing knowledge about games to play and fascinating things to do.

The nursery itself had been partitioned off to provide living quarters for the caretaker, as well as classrooms for us children, including his three. Mom would not let us visit them in their rooms, but we were allowed to play in school and outside with Denise, who was roughly our age, and Lucille and Leo, who were a year or two older. They got along with us, and we reveled in their company. We learned how to join in their games. We tasted something of the rough-and-tumble of childhood. We spent every possible minute with them, until the doleful day came when, for reasons unknown to us, the Chalifoux family packed up its belongings and drove on to another town and another job.

We were sure that nothing could ever be half as much fun again, but the next caretaker, Mr. Leblanc, brought along something else that was new and wonderful, and different from anything we had experienced. His wife was the mother of a baby less than twelve months old. Mrs. Leblanc had no hesitation about letting us play with her. We took turns cuddling her, bathing her, loving her. She was in grave danger of being worn out completely by our attentions.

The question of our education remained a puzzle until Dad came up with a brain wave. At least, he claimed that the new arrangement was his idea, though it would have been subject, naturally, to the approval of Church and state. We could go to boarding school, after all, provided the nursery building could be made over once more. True, we should not be separated, but then he did not want to see us separated. And we would be close at hand, under his eye. But together, constituting, among us, a good proportion of any class, we could live away from home.

Workmen tackled the job of converting the nursery for its new function. They sawed and hammered away through one summer to add a dormitory and have the place ready for its opening at the start of the school year as the Villa Notre Dame. "It was impossible to enroll the Quintuplets in a regular school," Dad explained, for publication. "This way they can continue their education as far as they wish. They will have the normal companionship of girls their own age without being deprived of the home atmosphere and home protection."

The new boarding school continued to be run by the Sisters of the Assumption. It was they who hand-picked the ten girls who were to be our fellow students. So that they would not feel that they were accepting charity, they were charged a small fee for their schooling. All the costs of making over the nursery and operating the Villa Notre Dame were borne by Quintuplet funds at the rate of $72,000 a year. A fine, wise man was installed as the first chaplain; on convalescent leave from Ottawa, Father Marcel Bélanger spent a full year there before he moved on to other duties.

At the start of the school year, we left the Big House behind us and took ourselves back to the old, familiar building which, transformed as it was, represented hope and happiness. The dormitory, with its hard beds and sparse furnishings, was a duplicate of any boarding-school dormitory, but we thought it was wonderful. In

122

one overwhelming respect, we were better off than ever before. Now we had human beings of our own age to have fun with, to tell us the perpetually intriguing story of how other people lived beyond Corbeil, beyond anywhere we could think of. We hung on every word they said, storing it away like five goblins hoarding gold.

We boarded with the other girls, ate with them, studied with them, slept in the same dormitory. We were all up at six-thirty every morning. Then Mass in the chapel before classes began at eight-thirty. With ninety minutes off for lunch and half an hour in the afternoon, we worked until six o'clock, and there was homework to be done in the evenings, too. But we wanted nothing better. We would not have minded in the least if we spent seven days a week at the Villa Notre Dame. We visited the Big House only when we had to, at weekends. Given our choice, we would not have gone there at all.

It was a state of affairs that Dad could not allow to continue.

For reasons not hard to find, Mom had an unshakable distrust of nurses and doctors ever since we could remember. For his part, Dad developed even more intense suspicions of priests and nuns. It is unlikely that he could have believed the tales himself, but he passed on to us all the ancient slanders of impropriety that haunt the history of the Church. As for the men and women concerned with instructing us, he hadn't a kind word to say for them. "They are leading you morally farther and farther away from your parents," he warned us. "They are out to divide the family again."

It was not in Dad's nature to say these things to a priest's face, but the chaplain at the Villa Notre Dame was a perceptive man. He seemed to know, without being told, what was being drummed into us at home. His response was to repeat over and over again the timeless message of his faith: "You must be patient. You must not pass judgment on your parents. Try to understand them. It is important to learn to forgive. Only in forgiving can you be forgiven."

Dad placed his trust in nobody. He convinced himself that as boarders we were exposed to bad influences, learning things that could only do us harm. At the end of the first year, he took us out of the Villa Notre Dame. For the second time, we were bundled off to the Big House, reluctantly, with heavy hearts. From now on, Dad ruled, we would go to classes there, but we would sleep at home.

Suspicious as he was of the hold that the nuns might have over us, he had equal doubts about another priest who came often to the scene. From the same order as Father Bélanger, the Oblates of Mary Immaculate, came Father Gustave Sauvé, who had been assigned by the government in Ottawa to give the Dionnes his care and attention.

He had been visiting us for years, seldom arriving empty-handed, never without something special to say from the depths of his wisdom. When we were still living in the nursery, he brought us a white rabbit one Eastertime. In the Big House, he turned up with movies to be shown in the playroom. This was one pleasure, watching movies, that was rarely questioned by Dad, so long as all the family was in the audience, together with some of the neighbors, too.

But he blamed Father Sauvé for influencing us against him. He seemed to feel that the priest was part of some dreadful conspiracy to keep the Dionnes divided against each other and set us apart from our parents. There was no basis for this, any more than for his imagining misdeeds at the Villa Notre Dame. One priest echoed the counsel of the other: "Be patient. Lead good lives. Keep charity in your hearts."

124

It would have been much better for us to be sent away, and better for Mom and Dad, too. If only we could have spent the next, troubled years in schools somewhere as distant as possible from Corbeil, so many problems might have been avoided. Mom and Dad would have been spared the torment of living with a situation that, with the best will in the world, could be improved only by the slow passage of time. We should have had the chance to continue meeting fresh faces, acquiring confidence in ourselves and knowledge of everyday things.

The boarders at the Villa continued to have a lot of fun. It was always a happy place, where we danced and joked in recreation periods and chattered and laughed at every other opportunity. We envied them when the school day was over and we made our way to the Big House, standing forbiddingly in its somber dark-yellow paint on the hilltop.

Once inside the front door, we had our chores to do. They waited for us in the morning, before we went off together to school. We tackled the house cleaning at that hour, washing floors, making beds, waxing furniture, leaving ourselves only a minute or two to scramble into our school uniforms and snatch up our homework books. More than anyone else, Marie was saddled with work, perhaps because she complained about it the least. Our brothers and sisters were allowed to leave half an hour or more ahead of us. The list of jobs that Mom assigned us was always considerably longer than theirs.

She took a hand, to the best of her ability, in our education. Puzzling over what the future might hold for us, she came to the conclusion at one time that she wanted each of us to become a writer. She herself was not a great reader, but something she had read impressed her with the virtues of writing as a profession. As practice for the craft, she instructed us to keep daily diaries so that we would develop the habit of putting words onto paper. The more we wrote each day, the better she was pleased.

But we were faced with a grave handicap. No matter how we wracked our brains, we had nothing to write about. Very little happened that seemed worth the paper it was to be recorded on. All we could think to do was race through our household labors, then pull out the diaries and hastily scribble such mundane entries as: "This morning I scrubbed the bathroom floor"; or "My turn to do the breakfast dishes."

For lack of anything else to enter, Annette once wrote that in playing with one of the watchdogs, she had noticed there were nipples under its fur. Was there a scene when Mom read that! Her standards of modesty were strict. This was an outrageous item to put into a diary. Anything having to do with relations between the sexes or procreation was not to be discussed under any circumstances.

It caused some rare difficulties when Mom was carrying the last of her children, Claude, who was born when she was thirty-seven and we were twelve. Pregnancy as a subject was obviously unmentionable. When it grew evident that she was going to have another baby and impossible to disguise the fact any longer, Dad took it on himself to break the news to us. It must be said that we had reached some conclusions of our own, since country-bred children are never totally unfamiliar with the ways of nature, by the time Dad loaded us into the car and took us for a drive. While we wound our way along miles of quiet roads that ran between the bleak fields and woodlands, he talked literally about the flowers and the bees. We managed to decipher what he meant and felt glad, in spite of some embarrassment, that he had taken us into his confidence.

Later, with many blushes and hesitations, Mom steeled herself to inform us about what she knew as the

126

facts of life. We were called into her bedroom, where she sat herself in her rocking chair with a marriage manual lying open in her lap. It was a distressing duty, which she would not allow herself to shirk. She carefully read to us what the author had to impart, and that was the sum total of instruction. We had as little desire to ask any questions as she would have had to answer them.

Though appearances counted a great deal with Mom, she had some strange ideas about what was proper in our appearance when we went to school. One morning a schoolmate appeared with her hair done up in two tight braids. When news of this reached Mom, she decided that we must follow suit. She kept us in pigtails for what seemed like years, and there was not a day when we did anything but hate them.

Another memory occurs of her experiments with the appearance we made in class. For some reason, she had us dab on lipstick, which she must have supplied, since we were strangers to cosmetics. We turned up in class with carmine lips, with the effect that could have been expected when the nuns saw us. We beat a retreat to the washroom and emerged with lips wiped clean and cheeks pink with shame.

When Mr. Leblanc, his wife and baby left the caretaker's quarters, our brother Ernest inherited the job. Working with Dad, he kept the lawns and flower beds around the Villa in immaculate condition. He very soon was engaged to a young schoolteacher in Corbeil, Jeannette Guindon, and Dad dearly wanted us to be bridesmaids at the wedding. The old fear of allowing the world to close in on us arose again, however, which decided him against holding the ceremony in the Corbeil church. Instead, Ernest and Jeannette were married in the little private chapel of the old nursery. According to the report that Dad gave *The Nugget*, it was our choice to wear ankle-length dresses with black velvet bodices, five of a kind. Of course, they had been bought without consulting us. The effect was perhaps theatrical and out of keeping with the ceremony, but the newspaper photographers gathered around. We would have preferred to stay in the background and leave the day for the bride.

The newlyweds set up housekeeping first in the upstairs quarters that the Leblancs had left empty. Then, when the nuns moved out of the staff house to move into the now converted Villa Notre Dame, Ernest and Jeannette transferred to the staff house. The furniture had to be carried from their old home to the new. There was a lot of fetching and carrying to be done, too, of food from the Big House kitchen and storehouse. Much of the work fell to the former bridesmaids. Fortunately there were plenty of us to help.

Dad felt no need to apologize to anyone who wondered how our time was spent, now that we had rejoined the family. "My daughters," he declared, "are only now beginning to lead normal, happy and private lives. The excitement which attended them at every turn during their first years is giving place to the quiet pursuit of studies which will fit them for a place in society." The two dollars a week that we each received as spending money was earned in perspiration. We used to believe that the money came out of Dad's pocket.

North Bay had three movie theaters—it still has at this writing—and they changed their programs twice a week. There came a time when Dad was seized by the movie-going habit. Six nights a week, we found ourselves being driven off to see a show, with sad consequences to our homework. Two or three classmates from the Villa were usually invited to join the party.

The back seat of the Cadillac Dad owned had developed trouble in its springing, apparently, and had been removed for repairs. The crowd of girls had no choice but to squeeze into the front. A sense of shyness was deeply rooted in all five of us. Sitting on laps, having arms around our shoulders and elbows in our ribs offended our susceptibilities. No matter if the evening was warm or chilly, we wrapped ourselves up in topcoats for protection on those outings to the movies, and no power on earth could persuade us to remove them. It has left an odd aftereffect in that nowadays only Yvonne has learned to drive a car.

Some excursions away from the Big House were more to our liking, though there were not so many of these after the journey to Ottawa to meet King George. At eight, we had seen a glimpse of the United States at Superior, Wisconsin, when we were asked to launch a Lend-Lease ship apiece there, with Niagara River water and not champagne in the bottles we swung against the bows.

We still have the plaques they gave us as souvenirs at the shipyard, but it is as though they belonged to another age. The observation car of the train we rode down from North Bay in was turned into a chapel on wheels, with flowers and a big candle, chalice and missal, so that we could honor Mom's birthday on May 7, while we were traveling. There were crowds all along the route, but we were not allowed to spend much time waving to them. We sang "God Bless America" and "There'll Always Be An England" on the radio, and that was that.

Four years went by before we made another excursion. With Father Sauvé and the rest of the family, we went to Ottawa for the Marian Congress, which was celebrating the hundredth anniversary of the Ottawa diocese. That produced more photographs for the scrapbooks, including a happy picture of Claude, a chubby baby, held in the arms of the Archbishop of Trivandrum, Monsignor Mar Ivanios, fascinated by the priest's flowing black beard.

More time passed, and we made a trip to New York

with eleven other girls from the Villa, to make an appearance and sing some songs at the Alfred E. Smith Memorial Foundation Dinner, where 2,500 guests paid a hundred dollars a plate to raise funds for charity. There was gossip about our first high-heeled shoes, worn for the occasion with our blue dresses. The nuns had bought them in North Bay, unseen by us.

The five days spent in New York brought some mixed moments. We should have liked to see much more of the city, but the timetable could not be stretched. There was an opportunity one afternoon to hurry off to the Statue of Liberty, but we had to forgo it. Dad wanted to meet Margaret O'Brien, instead; she was a big name in the movies then. But the meeting could not be arranged, so we were all disappointed for one reason or another.

Aboard the train leaving Grand Central Station, Dad got mad. We had made the mistake of waving through the windows at the crowds and signing autograph books that were thrust into our hands. Dad did not like to see us in the spotlight like that. We said silent farewells to the city while he read us a lecture on the errors of our ways.

Instead of going straight back to North Bay, we stopped off in Montreal to meet Monsignor Paul-Emile Leger, Archbishop of Montreal, and recite the Rosary with him on his evening radio show. Windsor Station there was swarming with crowds. They broke through the barriers the police had set up, and we were hustled off into hiding in the baggage room. The trick did not work, and the throng soon tracked us down, pressing against the windows to wave and call out greetings. This time we knew better than to wave back, but our classmates, who were traveling with us, enjoyed the fun.

A reporter tackled Dad, to ask whether we had enjoyed the trip. Dad was weary of it all. "You can see for yourself," he snapped.

As we all left the Archbishop's palace, another reporter had a few words with Pauline; we were kept out of reach. "I wouldn't be my sisters for anything," she said, and there was no doubt she meant it.

Dad was still upset by the jostling even after we arrived home. As he reprimanded us for the dozenth time, Marie made the mistake of talking back to him. For that, she had to go down on her knees and stay there until supper was ready.

What if we did have high heels and were sixteen? We were not thought of as being anything but children. We could not be permitted to grow up, because that would only complicate the problem of what was to be done with us. We were still urged to prove that we loved our parents, and that created more tensions than before.

EIGHT

ONE MORE YEAR PASSED, and then another, but very little changed for us. We were going on eighteen now, an age when most girls' thoughts have turned toward romance. We were not like that. Sure enough, there had been much talk in the newspapers about boy friends. "They haven't time for them," Dad said.

The truth was that we knew no boys to have as friends, except a cousin or two who sometimes came in to dance in the playroom, and the curly-haired baker's boy in his dashing, dark leather jacket, who used to deliver bread and willingly served as our secret messenger service.

Our brothers and sisters could write and receive any number of letters unscrutinized by either Mom or Dad, but we could not. All our correspondence, coming in or going out, was subject to being opened and read. If we wanted to send a note to a classmate during vacation, for instance, it had to be handed surreptitiously to the baker's boy, our one and only contact with the outside who could be relied upon to tell no tales.

We had survived one more public appearance, to greet another royal visitor to Canada. When Princess Elizabeth (as she was then) and the Duke of Edinburgh stopped off briefly at North Bay, we were lined up outside a hangar at the airport to say hello. It struck us as an incongruous setting—the concrete runways cracked by frost, the nondescript terminal building with its paint fading, the wilderness of scrub pines on every side, and the sign proclaiming that this was North Bay, elevation 1,213 feet.

We wore red hats brighter than the carpet that was unrolled shortly before the royal plane landed and taxied around to where the reception committee was waiting. Following instructions, we handed her a photograph of ourselves, feeling ill at ease over the inappropriateness of such a gift for such an occasion. In a magnificent mink coat, the Princess looked unimpressed. She said, "Hello," and that was about it. The Duke was much more outgoing, speaking both French and English and proving to be completely charming. We were greatly impressed by his clear skin and his keen blue eyes.

Annette was smitten by a sudden, irrelevant memory of what had happened when we met royalty before. As a red convertible took the Princess and the Duke off on a brief tour of the city—red was the color scheme for everything that day—she murmured, "Perhaps what Princess Elizabeth really wanted to tell us was, 'Now don't you kiss my husband, because he's mine!' "

The high heels came out of our closets for a second airing when we were invited to the winter carnival at St. Paul, Minnesota, as guests of the calendar manufacturers, who had been spreading Quintuplet pictures around by the millions for the past eighteen years.

We were no more familiar with three-inch heels than we had been at the Al Smith dinner in New York. During all the months that had gone by since then, we had

had no occasion to wear them. So, for days before the trip, we took ourselves off to our rooms, closed the doors and stumbled around like stilt-walkers, getting the feel of the heels, until our calves and ankles ached. We flattered ourselves that this rehearsing had prepared us for whatever might come our way; but we were mistaken.

A young man had been provided for each of us as an escort in St. Paul. After riding on a sleigh in a procession through the city, we changed into long evening dresses, five of the same kind again, for an appearance at the local stadium to see the carnival show. We were uniformly nervous but delighted to be out in the company of boys. One young man seemed to have eyes for nobody but Cécile, who had no more idea than the rest of us what to do about that.

To reach our places on the platform, we had to negotiate a steep and long flight of steps in full view of the crowd. In the trailing skirts and still wobbly heels, we might have managed it if only we had been given the sense to let go of our escorts' arms. But we had always been completely dependent on being told what to do. Holding on to the boys had been approved in advance, and nobody had told us not to cling and keep clinging. With the skirts threatening to trip us at every step, we floundered up the stairs like salmon struggling to swim up over a dam.

That night a grand ball was held as part of the celebrating, but this was judged to be unsuitable for us. Dad was our chaperon on the trip, along with Richard Donnelly, his attorney from North Bay, while Mom stayed home. We were sent to bed early, without being permitted to dance a step. Nevertheless, it was a wonderful experience, something that we could gossip about for months to come. For the first time, we had met some boys who struck us as being most attractive. And—dare we even admit it to each other?—we had been thrilled to

134

the core when they held our hands. If this was how ordinary people behaved, then we were unanimously in favor of it.

Something else happened in our days at the Villa Notre Dame that marked another modest step forward, out of darkness. We had new names for each other. They originated somehow under the inspiration of the Sister Superior, Sister Aimée des Anges, whose beaming face and kindly eyes behind her round, steel-framed spectacles brought a sense of peace when we were in her presence. The names are still in use among us, often employed in preference to those we were given at christening. They are a kind of bond, a badge of the "club," and a token of individuality, if that is possible.

Marie was called "Peewee," Emilie became "Em" and Cécile "Cis." Yvonne delighted to be known henceforth as "Ivy," and Annette thought "Netta" had a charm all its own. Hearing something about this process of renaming, Dad imagined that he too had been given a new identification. He thought that we were in the habit of referring to him as the Old Man, and he hated it. But he was mistaken. We did not speak of him in slighting terms. The other children sometimes called him that; not us.

We reached eighteen, as callow as ever, and the time came for the Villa to be shut down, its purpose served. The high-school era was over. Now we had to be placed somewhere else. Something else had to be tried, in the same spirit of doubt on every side that there was any chance of happiness in the outcome. We had our new names as a private legacy to take away with us, but little more than that. As scholars, we had not distinguished ourselves. Five places somewhere near the bottom of the class were our usual achievement when examinations came around.

We graduated from the Villa and celebrated our

birthday simultaneously. Dad had the stage set up again in the playroom of the Big House. In identical white gowns and white mortarboards, we marched up there with nine other classmates to receive our diplomas, while Dad, Mom and all eight of our brothers and sisters sat in the audience. The day lingers on with a special quality of its own in memory. It was the only time in our lives that we can recall Dad saying, "I am really proud of you."

It came as such a surprise that we were at a loss for any reply. We had no experience of praise. We glanced at each other and said nothing. He has never used those words to us again, and the fault cannot be considered wholly his.

In most subjects we were rated as no more than "fair" and in arithmetic positively "poor." Somehow we had squeaked through Latin and history, though not everyone remained wide-awake during those classes. A certain amount of nudging went on sometimes when a teacher's back was turned.

When it came to languages, we could speak English as fluently as French, and any dispute about our being instructed equally in both had long since faded into the past. Annette played the piano with some skill and was easily the best of us in music, as she had been all along. Yvonne showed promise of becoming something more than an amateur painter, though Dad did not care to hang her paintings in the Big House; he preferred those that Pauline did. Em, concealing her attacks from everyone but the family, had grown into the most soberminded of us, while Cécile was the most outgoing personality and Mom's indisputable favorite. Yvonne was still the natural leader, the most serious and the most scared. Marie to all outward appearance was the most docile, but out of sight and within her soul a great change was in the making.

In spite of what we could read in the newspapers

about the careers we were supposed to be in training for, we had, in fact, received no practical experience whatever. If we had been compelled to begin earning a living when we graduated, we should have been judged as unemployable.

Instruction at the Villa had been concentrated on the side of religion, not on any thought of our ever needing a job. This was a great joy to Mom, whose faith is devout, single-minded and unshakable. Mass was said every morning in the chapel in the old staff house. Evening prayers, weather permitting, were said by the statue of the Virgin in the little grotto at the back of the Big House. On every feast of the Virgin, we had to put out a statue of Her indoors and dress it with flowers.

At most of the public appearances we made, a point invariably came in the program where we would join in prayers and recite the Rosary. We collected more presentation prayer books and rosaries than we could use or even remember. Mom must have added them to her own collection, which could not grow too large to please her. We seldom saw them again once we got home.

Throughout the day, as schoolgirls at the Villa, we were encouraged to murmur little prayers to ourselves, as nuns and priests do. On Friday afternoons, we were put to the task of making scrapbooks, dozens of them, of holy pictures, cutting out the figures and pasting them in elaborate compositions of our own on the pages. It would have been an excellent pastime for little children, but we could well have been allowed to develop abilities beyond that.

"I think there was too much of what is superficial in religion around us," Cécile has said. "Surely the love of God should not be taught in the way a soldier is drilled, but as a choice of free will that is made both in the mind and in the heart. When you are in trouble, you find it is not a scrapbook that you think of."

But the Church and its representatives had seen and understood more than we realized then about our circumstances. We were taken under its wings for protection in many ways. We did not forget that. What feelings of security there were within us came mostly from the Church's help, though the feelings often faltered in those days. Without the watchful presence of the priests and nuns, it would have been much more difficult to survive with some measure of dignity in life.

Nicolet is a quiet, old-fashioned town of perhaps five thousand people that stands on the steep, red-clay banks of the Nicolet River where it empties into the massive St. Lawrence River. It is a town of neat frame houses set on tree-lined streets. A tannery and woodworking factories were situated there, but the flavor of the place was established not by industry but by the dominating presence of the Cathedral of St. Jean Baptiste with its towering twin spires, and by the two monasteries in town, the convent, the religious schools for boys and girls, and the Institut Familial, a Catholic college for girls conducted along the strictest old-fashioned lines. Nicolet is in the Province of Quebec, which means that French is spoken much more than English in its streets and homes.

When Dad told us that we had been enrolled at the Institut for the new school year, beginning in September, our spirits soared. At long, long last we should be set free from seclusion and confinement. We five were going to be by ourselves again, happy in the company of each other, without the stresses and strains that family living seemed constantly to impose.

And then the reaction inevitably struck us. What would it be like to live away from home, exposed to situations we might not be able to cope with? Would we feel safe outside the walls that had been built around us from the very beginning? We were as timid as deer.

We spent many sleepless hours speculating about the strange and perhaps hostile future that appeared to be opening up for us. We had no experience of any kind to draw on, so some of our thoughts took strange turns. Though no crowd or stranger had ever harmed us, or attempted to, we had been taught that anything and anybody beyond our tight little sphere was dangerous, to be avoided like the plague. We had been brought up to talk very seldom, except to each other, and then only when we were spoken to. We did not know how to cross a street alone or to buy so much as a handkerchief, or to do anything of our own volition.

We developed the wild fancy that we should run into serious trouble at Nicolet if anybody recognized us. We wondered how we might conceal ourselves by choosing other names, by walking only in twos and threes because the five of us would create too great a stir. Cécile and Annette concocted a cunning scheme to dye their hair auburn as a disguise. They spent a busy evening together over a hand basin in one of the bathrooms, following the instructions on the bottle step by step. But the project had to be abandoned; all they succeeded in dying was their hands.

The courses prescribed for us at the Institut covered home economics, languages, music, elocution, psychology, literature, dietetics, physics, chemistry and decorative arts. The same order of nuns, the Sisters of the Assumption, conducted the Institut as had run the Villa. Dad drove us down from Corbeil, making it a point to arrive late in the day so that our arrival would attract the least possible attention.

Half pleased, half disappointed, we found that the pattern had changed only little. Instead of the transformation we had both feared and hoped for, life at the Institut bore a close resemblance to what we had known before. The difference was in being away from the Big

House, but we still spent hour after hour learning how to sew fine seams, trace ornamental designs on wood with heated irons and do intricate embroidery.

Unknown to us were the special instructions that Dad had given the nuns in charge. All the fees for our studies were paid for out of Quintuplet funds, and our spending money came from the same source. Yet we each received only two dollars a month. That made us paupers compared with most of the other girls. We could not make out the Mother Superior's meaning when she told us one day, "You are rich enough to buy the entire college if you cared to." The sheer existence of the money banked in the Quintuplet name was a subject on which we had no information at all. We were certain that everything came out of Dad's pocket.

We eked out our allowances to the best of our ability until one of us plucked up the courage to mention our straits to the Mother Superior. The interview had us all trembling at the prospect of the trouble we feared we might be causing. But the Mother Superior did what we dared not do. On our behalf, she asked Dad for more money. We were overjoyed to have our allowances raised to five dollars.

Some of the discoveries we made at Nicolet were disconcerting. It dawned on us, for example, that we were comparatively small in stature when the only wall mirrors in which we could see ourselves were those in the basement locker rooms. We went down there when we could, but most mornings, as we washed hands and faces, we had to tackle our hair with the help of pocket mirrors. We must have looked like the tousled Dionnes much of the time, and we wanted so badly to make a good impression.

Annette had a personal daydream that remained with her for years. She would picture herself being a tall, stately woman—five feet eight inches from top to toe at the very least—who could see herself in any mirror and therefore, perhaps, win universal respect and consideration.

It may have been the result of unduly sensitized imaginations and self-doubts, but we were convinced that the nuns were habitually sterner with us than with any of the other students. It was as if they were silently impressing on us a special lesson: "You must learn to expect no favors here merely because you are Quintuplets. The sooner you appreciate that, the better it will be."

We were uncomfortably aware of being always watched. The family had kept us under surveillance before; now it was the nuns. We had hoped to escape from such close observation, but this was not to be. To us, this meant that any imperfections in our conduct would be reported straight back to Dad. There was still that finger in the back to say "Sit up straight" and "Behave yourselves."

The rules prohibited having locks on the drawers where our clothes and few personal belongings were kept in our rooms. Suitcases stored down in the basement also had to remain unlocked and open for inspection at any time. The only secrets one could guard were those within oneself.

On Dad's instruction, we were not allowed to leave the premises for any reason. On Sunday afternoons, when the other girls could receive visitors and go into the town if they had a parent's approval, we were escorted to one of the classrooms and locked in until visiting hours were over. The time dragged by so slowly, while from the other side of the door came the tantalizing sounds of classmates enjoying themselves.

The hours were supposed to be spent in writing letters, but we had nobody to write to except Mom and Dad. With them, every word put down on paper had to be weighed and reweighed, examined for every possible shade of meaning. Dad was a great one for reading between the lines. The letters could not be too short, or he would feel slighted, nor too glib, or he would suspect we were keeping things from him, nor too gay, because he did not regard life as a matter for jokes. We wrote in French. He always replied in English.

Once the weekly duty notes had been folded into their envelopes, one from each of us, each saying much the same things, there was nothing to do but try to read, wander around the desks or stare blankly through the windows, counting off the minutes until supper would be served and we should be released.

Yet, on the whole, we were happy enough in Nicolet. We roomed together in a blue-and-green dormitory. We could study together and eat together and share our thoughts without too much interference. So we always had each other's company, and that was really what we needed to give the days a little warm glow.

NINE

THE BREAK came on our next birthday, eight months later. The first of us to attempt an entirely new and different existence by an act of her own decision was Marie. She was the most timid and the least sturdy, yet it was she, according to what the nurses had said, who showed the most determined will to live when we were only a matter of hours old.

On the day we reached nineteen, Mom and Dad drove down to Nicolet to spend the birthday with us in a cottage close by the Institut which the nuns put at our disposal for the occasion. At that meeting, Marie announced her news, once the ritual of press photographs had been concluded.

"I am going to enter a convent and serve God," she said. "I have thought of it for a long time. I have prayed, and I have decided."

Dad's thoughts were impossible to read. His face was inscrutable. But Mom was overjoyed that a child of hers should choose to be a religious. There was no question of opposing Marie. In point of fact, in the years ahead,

143

Oliva junior spoke of becoming a priest and Pauline took the veil four times as a postulant, but they did not go further than that.

A Catholic child, particularly a girl, will often dream of taking holy orders. It is a kind of romantic affair with God, bearing many of the marks of adolescent love. She sees the example set by the nuns in her church, and perhaps at school, in their service to God. She sometimes mistakes the stirrings that accompany the change from child to woman for the deeper desire. All of us had the same dream, but there was a notable difference between our case and that of many girls raised under more usual conditions. The nuns around us continually implanted the thought that we should find it easier to follow in their steps. "It would be simpler for you than for most," they said.

If it is true that of the vows of poverty, chastity and obedience, the key to sanctity is obedience, we had all been well schooled. We had been brought up, like nuns, to have a predetermined time to wash ourselves, sleep, eat and pray as a matter of instinct throughout the day. We knew so little of the world that it would not be difficult to give that little up.

There was a more important consideration for us than any of that. To enter a convent meant escaping from the existence we led, which we realized more and more clearly was an unnatural one holding no promise of future happiness. Neither we nor those responsible for us had any idea what was to become of us. Not that the question lacked public discussion. Thousands and thousands of words were written about it, and some of them make ironic reading. We had "more than earned the right to freedom of choice as to their futures," according to one author. Another concluded that our lives had been regulated "in such a manner as to train them to appreciate the fullness of living rather than to capitalize upon their uniqueness."

We were too shut off from true reality to appreciate, except in what seemed to be the wildest fancies, that more than two choices lay open to us. We were sure that we must either return some day to live on in the Big House, pent up there until we became old maids, or enter the Church. Those were the only alternatives facing us. So the decision for Marie was not nearly as hard as it would have been for girls with a different history. The nuns who taught us had spoken the simple truth. In some degree, four of us came later on to a similar discovery.

Before Dad confided Marie's plan to the newspapers, he let three months go by. It was not like him to keep back an announcement as important as this, which could be depended upon to make headlines, but he had a lot to think about before he could arrange his thoughts in proper order.

"For several years now," he said, once he had decided what to say, "little Marie has been developing an idea which she did not dare discuss with her mother and father in case they would object. As I have always done in the past, every decision was made for the girls' own benefit. Therefore, once more I don't feel I should interfere with Marie's intimate desire."

The summer had come and gone before Marie finally left home. We had all been there from the time the school year ended at Nicolet. Three of us—Em, Cécile and Annette—returned for a second year at the Institut, since we could effectively do nothing else. But Yvonne did not. The slow stirring of independence, owing much to Marie's stanchness, was in our minds. Yvonne found it irresistible, while it took longer to work on us. She wanted no more of the Institut Familial. She was determined to go alone to Montreal to enter College Marguerite Bourgeois as an art student.

It turned out that she had an unexpected ally who eased the way for her. Dad did not fight against her leaving. Pauline, who had studied at Marguerite Bourgeois herself, used her influence with him to make things easy for Yvonne. It was a quiet departure, so smoothly arranged that nobody was upset over it. She did not return to live at the Big House after that.

Marie's leave-taking was something else. By now the rest of us were already either at Nicolet or, in Yvonne's case, starting a new era in Montreal. None of us went home to say goodbye to Marie. Dad handled it impressively. The photographers were invited in for a special session, posed in advance just as it might have been in nursery days. Mom and Dad bidding farewell to Marie on the front steps of the house. Mom helping her with her packing. Marie kneeling on the living-room rug while Dad raises his hands over her head and blesses her in the French custom.

Marie was urged to explain to reporters. "I am grateful for those many prayers that people throughout the world said for us when we were babies," she said. "From now on my prayers will be offered up for others."

A week before her departure, the relatives and neighbors were invited over for open house by Dad, which brought a fresh round of stories in the newspapers. On the day that Marie went to Quebec, the newsmen swarmed around like bees. She was going into one of the strictest orders, the Servants of the Very Holy Sacrament, whose members join in perpetual prayer, each taking turns to kneel in the chapel for three hours out of every twenty-four.

"I care nothing for the things of the world," she said, in all truth at that time. "I feel that I belong in a convent. It is the only place where I can be happy."

Yvonne came from Montreal, Cécile and Annette from Nicolet, to be there in Quebec City, the ancient, walled fortress of French Canada which stands like a monument to past glories. Em was absent. In an attack of epilepsy the day before, she had fallen and hurt her ankle and shoulder. She stayed behind in the Institut infirmary, weeping to see her two sisters leave as she would surely have wept for Marie. Dad did not make the journey to Quebec either. Our brother-in-law, Maurice Girouard, who had been married to Rose-Marie in the new Sacred Heart Church in Corbeil four years earlier, drove Marie down with Mom.

In the little reception hall of the yellow stone convent, the nuns formed a double row of greeting. Their faces were every bit as solemn as ours. We waited tensely in the sparsely furnished visitors' parlor while Marie, out of sight and helped by the novices, fumbled her way into the unfamiliar black cotton caped dress of a postulant and laced up the heavy, thick-soled shoes.

She would have to spend six months here, where a year or a decade or a century was an almost meaningless measurement of time, before she was promoted to novice. During this period of testing and examination of and by herself, she would be under rigid supervision by the professed nuns.

With the long white veil over her short hair, she came quietly into the parlor for a little while to say goodbye. None of us in the room could begin to express what was in our hearts. A few commonplace words that none of us can remember sufficed to pass the few remaining minutes. We all started with smiles and finished in tears and kisses before the black wooden grille was opened and Marie turned through it and was gone.

For all we knew, she would never again leave this cloister, one of many in the old city whose narrow, winding streets she would not see. She must learn here to live only by the book called the Holy Rule, which governed every moment of the day. As we walked away, clustered together for need of human warmth and touch, it seemed inconceivable that she would be spending the rest of her years behind these walls, while we remained outside, able to visit her from time to time but never recapturing the faraway days when five of us played and laughed as one.

Marie slept on a straw mattress laid on planks of wood, in a tiny cubicle with a cotton draw curtain suspended from a rod over the doorway. The harsh, unbleached sheets were part of the discipline as well as a silent reminder of vows. Postulants were moved from cubicle to cubicle according to careful rule, so that none could feel a sentimental and therefore unworthy attachment to any special corner of the impersonal dormitory. This, too, was important in the diminishment of self, the surrender of one's own will to the supreme will of God.

The days were divided and dominated by the ringing of bells, which were to be interpreted as the voice of God Himself summoning them to duty and their devotions. Not to obey instantly and unquestioningly was an imperfection, and imperfections need be entered in a notebook reserved for that purpose which was part of the equipment of every postulant. She had very few possessions, but regulations did allow a single snapshot of her family.

She had to acquire the power of interior silence, the quietness of mind that stills frivolity. She had to learn the language of hands that replaced speech for all but thirty minutes each day after dinner and another thirty following supper; at other times, the movement of a hand or of fingers would convey every necessary "please" or "thank you" or "excuse me." During the permitted conversation period, talk must be confined to general topics. What happened in the past, before she was admitted to the convent, was not considered to be a suitable subject for a postulant to discuss. The submission of self to the will of God included walking always with hands concealed and eyes lowered to the ground, not even glancing out of a window toward the sky unless permission had been asked and granted.

Marie could write only two letters a month, but in theory she could receive as many as were sent to her. One or two arrived from Mom which the authorities intercepted and would not pass on to Marie, since they judged them to be too upsetting. Once again the specter of money, or the desire for it, was haunting the family. If Marie wanted to talk to the family, would she please place the calls to Corbeil from the convent and pay for them at her end? If she would like Mom to visit her in Quebec, she would be glad to make the trip if only Marie would send the price of the fare.

Four days before our twentieth birthday, Marie became Sister Marie-Rachel, a novice. She had been tested by her months as a postulant and found acceptable to the order. Dad came with Mom from Corbeil for the ceremony, Yvonne from Montreal and the other three of us from Nicolet. It marked the beginning of a further two years as a novitiate before finally Marie could be a professed nun.

In the small, modern Mount Thabor Chapel, Marie waited with four other postulants who had been admitted to the congregation at the same time as she. Father Wilfred Honoré La France, the priest of our Corbeil parish, made a special journey down to assist at the Mass and the benediction.

Until she read a card handed to her during the cere-

149

mony, Marie did not know what her new, religious name was to be; it was one of the five each postulant had chosen earlier and submitted to the Superior General. At the crucial part of the service, the newest novices filed out of the chapel while two professed nuns brought in a wicker basket containing the white wool gowns and sleeveless cotton scapulars, which symbolize the yoke that Jesus bore to Gethsemane. These vestments were blessed, then carried out again to the five girls who were waiting outside to dress in their new robes and return to the chapel for the conclusion of the Mass.

Afterward, we stood again in the visitors' parlor and watched impatiently for the dark wooden grille to open and admit Marie. There was a radiance in her face when she came in, making scarcely a sound as she entered. Mom and Dad had brought a present for her, an oil painting chosen by Pauline. It portrayed Jesus with Martha and Mary in the house of Lazarus; it was "The Best Choice." This was necessarily a token gift. Along with everything else she owned, it was due to become the property of the order. This time, at the conclusion of our visit, Marie walked back through the grille calmly and without a tear.

"I found the ceremony very touching," Dad said, "and I am very happy."

And then the same longing that had moved Marie had its effect on another of us, on Em. She had said only a little to the rest of us about it, but that was not unusual. As time slipped by, she had grown less and less communicative, more and more engrossed with an internal life of her own. She was unlike the other four of us in several ways. She was a soul apart, who cared nothing whatever for clothes or make-up or money, while we liked at least to talk about such things. None of us was encouraged to consider marriage as the remotest possibil-

150

ity, but we had a normal interest in the thought of romance in a fairy-tale sense. Em, to the contrary, genuinely had no interest in boys, never wore make-up, never spoke of marriage. Perhaps this was a consequence of her affliction; she may have decided that the only possible course for her would be to enter a convent. She had written in an essay once, "I prefer to remain a child in the woods and unattached. Nature means so much to me."

At the Institut, she had been studying Church history and the lives of the saints. She was greatly influenced by Father Louis-Marie Parent of the Oblates of Mary Immaculate, who had visited us often at the Villa Notre Dame. He had founded a rambling white hostel called L'Hospice de L'Accueil Gai up in the Laurentian Mountains two miles outside the winter resort of Ste. Agathe des Monts, in the Province of Quebec. It was a rest home conducted by seven Oblate nuns for aged clergy, and he was seeking recruits to the order.

Em applied to enter the convent at L'Accueil Gai, but it was a secret possibly known only to Mom and Dad. The other three of us—Cécile, Yvonne and Annette— were not told about it. When we arrived home with Em from Nicolet for the summer, while Yvonne stayed in Montreal, it was still a secret.

Another secret, that Em was an epileptic, was apparently kept from the nuns at L'Accueil Gai, though Mom felt certain that Father Parent would have mentioned it to them. In any event, Em went into the convent.

There was no fuss and no announcement about it. Dad said later, "She hadn't been quite herself during recent months. That is one of the reasons she went to Ste. Agathe to rest and where the air is good." Ostensibly she was going to judge whether she would want to be admitted as a postulant, following Marie's example. But in reality she was determined, before she left the Big House, to serve God as a nun for the rest of her days.

But in Quebec City, the rigors of her new identity as Sister Marie-Rachel had drained Marie's strength, despite her resolution to continue. She was too ill and too weak to remain with the Servants of the Very Holy Sacrament. Father Parent went to collect her and drove her to the town of Richelieu, across the Richelieu River, half an hour's journey from Montreal, where there is another Oblate convent. It seemed to have been his intention to take her there to rest and possibly regain some of her vitality. At Marie's request, he telephoned L'Accueil Gai. Marie wanted Em, the sister to whom she had always felt closest, the one who could best understand her plight in the present circumstances. Would Em please, if possible, come to Richelieu?

Em took the first available means of making the journey from Ste. Agathe; she caught a bus. In those days, when we were either confined at the Big House or secluded at Nicolet, none of us had traveled alone, and we had not the least idea of how to manage it. Riding on a bus was a bewildering experience for Em, the "child in the woods" who had never before set foot inside one unaccompanied. There were reports later saying that she had an attack on the bus, which travels forty-five miles to Montreal, then on for twenty miles more to Richelieu.

"Is it true that you were ill on the bus?" Cécile asked her.

Em was always aware if she had had a seizure. "No," she replied. "I was very confused, and I got out too soon—in Montreal, not Richelieu."

Montreal is a teeming city, the biggest, busiest and probably the noisiest in Canada. The streets are jammed with traffic, and the sidewalks overflow with people. At

152

night, neon signs blaze in the darkness, and the pace is as fast as it is by day. Em wandered through the city in a daze, utterly unused to such glare and such crowds, lost and much too ashamed of herself for being lost to summon her courage and ask the way. Finally, a patrol car picked her up and took her to a police station.

"They wanted me to spend the night there," she told Cécile. "They thought I was stupid. I did not want to tell them my name, because of the publicity it would bring. I made them promise first that they would not let anyone know if I told them I was a Quintuplet, but they broke their promise. They were not polite."

A police car took her to the palace of Cardinal Leger. This was not entirely unfamiliar to her, for we had, of course, visited here on our way back from New York. From there, a secretary of the Cardinal's escorted Em to the bus station from which she had wandered hours before, and he put her aboard the right bus for Richelieu.

But by this time the news was out. Once again the Montreal papers had a front-page story about the Quintuplets. In the Big House the telephone rang in Dad's study. "Is it true," the reporter asked, "that your daughter Emilie is spending the night in prison?"

Cécile had been staying with Rose-Marie and Maurice Girouard at their home in Waterloo. She was driving back to Corbeil with Oliva when the car radio blared out the bulletin that Marie was ill and had been taken to the convent at Richelieu, while Em had been picked up by the police in Montreal.

Oliva made immediately for Richelieu. Em had arrived there safely at last and had talked to Marie. Now they were waiting together, reassured by each other's presence, for someone to collect them both and take them on the next steps of their journeys. There was no debate about what should happen to Marie. She had to rest and rebuild her health, and the only thing for her to do was to let Oliva and Cécile take her to Corbeil. But Em would not hear of going home.

She was adamant; she must return straightway to Ste. Agathe. She wanted that more than anything, and nothing else would do for her. When Dad telephoned Richelieu and heard her plan, he took it as a direct affront. He demanded that, after the sensation caused in Montreal, she should come back under his wing.

In spite of his anger, Em was not to be argued with any longer. "I do not intend to go back home," she said as calmly as she could. "I am going into the convent, and I shall spend the rest of my life there."

This time, at least, Mom made certain that the nuns at L'Accueil Gai realized the truth about Em's health. Apparently they were amazed that she was an epileptic. But they took her back at L'Accueil Gai; the French name means "Happy Welcome." We felt confident that the nuns, accustomed as they were to caring for the old and sick, could be depended upon to watch over her. She had no more than two months to spend there.

The other four of us passed that summer at the Big House, restlessly trying to make plans for the future, facing the old, old problem of what to do next. We were all aware of the silent struggle that went on within each of us and with Dad. We fought against being pulled back into the dependent, docile habits that we were only just beginning to break. The sweet taste of independence, however limited it was as yet, was not to be forgotten. But Dad would have liked us to remain as we had been for so many years, alive only in his shadow.

On Thursday evening, August 5, Annette was alone with Mom, getting ready to walk down the road and do some baby-sitting for Ernest and Jeannette. It was not a particularly unusual way of spending an evening, and Mom had given no thought to being left alone. But suddenly, she could not bear the prospect. She is not a timid woman, but now she was plainly terrified. The time was close to eight o'clock.

"I can sense death in the air," she insisted, and there was no consoling her. Annette felt it would be wrong to leave her. She called off the baby-sitting and stayed home that evening.

◆§ TEN §◆

At ten o'clock the next morning, Dad received a telephone call from L'Accueil Gai. The voice of the nun was solemn at the other end of the line. "Your daughter Emilie is seriously ill," he was told. "She has had a stroke. If you would like to see her, you should come without delay."

He turned first to Father Sauvé, the priest whom he would not trust in less troubled times. As soon as Dad had finished speaking with the nun, he telephoned the priest in Ottawa, asking him to go to Em's side as soon as he possibly could, to arrive ahead of Dad. But it turned out that it was already too late for anyone to make the journey and see her alive.

One day earlier, we were subsequently informed, Em had been stricken at a picnic given in the grounds of the hostel for the dozen or so old people who were being cared for there. In her fall, she bruised an ankle. Em could judge her condition unfailingly. She must have sensed that a series of attacks might well follow in rapid succession after this. She would need someone with her

156

to help her when she lost consciousness. She asked that a nun sleep with her in the little gray-walled room where until then she had slept alone. It was our sister's last home.

Three more seizures convulsed her in the night, but of course she survived them. To inexperienced eyes, the attacks are alarming, but nobody is hurt by them, only by the accidents that can happen when control and consciousness are lost. In the morning, Em remained in bed, refusing any food, while everyone else in the hostel went as usual to Mass.

"I looked in on her before we went, and she was sleeping peacefully," one of the Oblates said later. "I thought she was all right."

That afternoon, early, another call came to the Big House from L'Accueil Gai. It was a blazing-hot day, tourist weather. A handful of men and women in thin shirts and bright dresses were picking over the souvenirs at Madame Legros's gift shop, which was still in business down the road. Mom and Dad were in the library, talking with two nuns in blue-gray habit, strangers to us, who had called to see him. The four of us, with Oliva and Victor, were in the middle of lunch in the dining room. Memory plays peculiar tricks when the world is shaken. The sight of the table comes back clear as day. There were blueberries for dessert. We were passing the sugar bowl and the cream pitcher from one to another when the telephone rang that second time.

The radio was playing, but Oliva went over to turn it off immediately Mom came into the room. The look on her face was all the sign he needed. She said nothing for a second or two, and then: "Take hold of yourselves. The nuns telephoned. Emilie has died."

It was not possible for that to be true, so the four of us could not accept what Mom had said. You could not have one die without the rest. How could we be alive if she was not? Yet we could do nothing but believe Mom. Together we stumbled upstairs, not knowing what we should say or might do.

Epilepsy by itself does not kill people. It did not kill Em. She died as a consequence of being alone, with no one at her side to take care of her. We never left her like that at home. The coroner explained that death came from suffocation; she was found face downward on her pillow, unable to turn her head for breath. An accident. Natural causes. The policemen who conducted an investigation found no signs of violence except the biting of her tongue, caused by the unchecked clenching of her teeth in the early stages of the attack.

The Oblate who directed the hostel talked to the newspapers. "I arrived in her room just a few minutes before she died. We had no idea she was so ill. When we did realize it, there wasn't time to get the doctor. She was unconscious when Father Omer Lavergne gave her the last rites."

Em was carried out of her room on a stretcher. Outside, in the sun, she was laid on the grass, with a red rug covering her. The nuns had tried to find a doctor who would come in to make an examination and sign the necessary death certificate. None would do so, though one had arrived and pronounced her dead. It was he who told the newspapers. It was five o'clock by the time the local coroner had arrived, to order an inquest after his examination of her. Then an ambulance was called to carry her from L'Accueil Gai, down the hill from which one sees the Rivière du Nord, into the town of Ste. Agathe itself.

In nine days more, she would have been accepted as a novice into the congregation of the Oblates, without serving the usual months as a postulant. She had proved herself to be so eager, so willing, so devoted that a special exception was to have been made for her. So far as the nuns were concerned, they regarded her as a Sister already. Seven of them went to the Ste. Agathe funeral parlor where she lay that night and wept while they prayed.

She was taken first to Montreal, fifty miles away, where an autopsy was performed. The doctor said she had only a few more years to live at most. The glands of her body were continually enlarging themselves, he said, and she would eventually have suffered great pain. She knew nothing of that, and neither did we.

All the nuns from the hostel were invited by Dad to the funeral, which was set for Monday morning in the Sacred Heart Church in Corbeil, built in the boom days when tourists by the hundreds of thousands streamed in to visit the Quintuplets. Father Parent came to the church, together with twenty other priests. But no Oblate came from L'Accueil Gai. Later, when Em's baggage was returned, her suitcases were battered and the locks had been broken. Her spectacles were shattered, too. We often wondered what had happened, and when, to cause such damage.

Rose-Marie and her husband had gone to Ste. Agathe to make the necessary identification of Em and to escort her home. For the first time, the world outside learned that Em had been an epileptic for most of her life, that the Dionnes, in spite of the publicity they had been subjected to, had managed to keep at least one secret locked inside the Big House.

The shiny black hearse set off on the long, dusty journey to Corbeil, three hundred miles away, with the Girouards following in their car. So that the party could eat something, the cars stopped in the little town of Pembroke, halfway along the road home. A group of nuns, driving by, recognized the sad procession. They stopped and fell to their knees in the Pembroke street. Soon other passersby joined them in their prayers.

159

It was dark before Em returned to the Big House, where a single vigil candle burned by the statue of the Virgin with the broken hand that stood on the window sill at the turn of the stairs. Outside the steel fence the crowds had started to gather by the hundreds. Now and then the gates were unlocked by one or another of our brothers to let a visitor in. Mort Fellman came, and Richard Donnelly. A man from the telegraph office in North Bay arrived to handle the dozens of telegrams that Dad was sending, with invitations to the funeral.

Even so soon as this, there was a plan in the making to establish a kind of memorial to Em. The two gray-habited nuns who had been visiting Dad when the second call came from L'Accueil Gai were missionary recluses of the Order of Jesus and Mary, founded in Montreal a dozen years earlier. Reverend Mother Rita-Marie, the founder, and her traveling companion had a request to make when they heard the news. They wasted little time about it.

"We offer you our deep sympathy in your loss," said the Reverend Mother, who went on to speak of a proposal for buying the old nursery, which had stood empty and neglected since its career as the Villa Notre Dame had come to an end. She would establish it as a monastery, she said, in memory of Em. "Your daughter would have been happy about that," she persuaded Dad. "She would have said Yes to us, I think."

Dad agreed on the spot not to sell but to hand over the place to the recluses. Nobody could have guessed then that it was the start of a new chain of events that surprised and dismayed us over the years ahead.

From the time Em came home that night until early the following morning, the four of us watched over her for the last time, grieving and still disbelieving that there was any truth in what we knew was true. Then we tried for a while to sleep, but before dawn we went downstairs again to the living room. She lay in a dress of blue, her special color ever since our nursery days, with a white crucifix and a Rosary between her fingers. A news agency photographer came in and snapped the final picture of the Quintuplets together, united and indivisible, five of a kind who on earth now numbered four. We fled upstairs again before the crowds began streaming in.

Not since the house was built, fourteen years before, had Dad unlocked the gates to everyone who cared to call. Now the gates and the house itself stood wide open, inviting and welcoming, in his words, "persons genuine in their grief." Thousands of people wound their way up the driveway, up the steps and through the house to take a last glance of respect, curiosity, who knows what, at her calm face showing above the black-and-gold shroud.

They say it was quite like old times in some ways. Cars filled the asphalt parking areas in the beating afternoon sun and spilled out onto the highway that the government put in twenty years earlier. Young and old waited in line for an hour and more. Tourists in sports shirts and blue jeans. Mothers with babies in their arms. Neighbors from nearby farms. Police guards patrolled the grounds and ushered the crowds in and out, but they were not needed. Cameras were not permitted, but nobody protested about that. Everything was quiet and orderly.

Mom and Dad took it as their duty to greet every caller with a word of welcome. "The way everyone has been so kind to us is more than we can express," he said. "We are very, very grateful."

The following morning, hundreds of tourists' cars lined the highway outside the house and every other road around Corbeil. They followed, bumper to bumper in an unbroken line, when Em was taken to the little red brick church. The sexton, blind old Albert Giroux, tolled the bell as the cortege drew near. The weather had broken, and the dark sky threatened rain. Father La France

161

offered Mass at the main altar, Father Sauvé at one side of the altar, Father Bélanger at the other. The church overflowed with people, whose eyes one wished to avoid. There was a sermon and no eulogy.

The graveyard is reached down a rough dirt road, half a mile from the church. It is set in a corner of a farmer's field with uncleared brush pressing in on the weathered headstones. There were bigger crowds waiting there. Reporters and photographers trampled down the coarse grass, which someone had hurried to cut just the day before. The four of us who were left trailed in behind Father La France and the altar boys who carried the Cross and the candles.

Em was lowered into a shallow grave that Ernest had helped to dig. It is the custom for each family to look after the graves of its own members. The brightest colors, brighter than the robes of the priests, came with the mound of flowers piled up beside the dug-up ground, close to the two gray crosses marking the place where our grandparents lay buried.

Within minutes, raindrops fell and then a torrent of rain. We were driven back to the Big House. We knew there must be something we could do in memory of Em. If it was impossible now, there would be a later day.

162

◄§ ELEVEN ε►

D AD took us to the railroad station in North Bay, and scarcely a word was spoken between us. He sat impassively at the steering wheel of the Cadillac, and we had long since been taught to mask our feelings as he did. As he must have done, we realized that after this leave-taking nothing could be the same again. The four survivors were going together to live in Montreal. In eight more months, we should be twenty-one years old. We should, of course, be returning to visit Mom and Dad, but in our hearts this was really adieu. We felt a strange mixture of fear and delight. But regret? Yes, deeply. We were still numbed at the thought that Em was not with us, and we were in mourning for her.

It was a matter-of-fact farewell for all that. We turned down Ferguson Street toward the Canadian Pacific tracks. We lifted out our bags and stood on the platform for a while, with its glimpse of Lake Nipissing showing over the freight yards, where a little locomotive fusses constantly to and fro. When the train pulled in, bell ringing, metal clanging, Dad said, "Goodbye then."

163

We said, "Goodbye. See you at Christmas." It had been much the same kind of thing at the house, leaving Mom.

The legends have it that we were unwilling to leave home, but the truth is that we were happy to go. When the train pulled out, we could take a deep breath and relax and chatter about this virtually unknown city of Montreal, which only Yvonne, from her year of studying at Marguerite Bourgeois, was even faintly familiar with.

It was to that college that Annette and Marie were going, Annette to study music so that perhaps one day she might become a teacher, Marie to take a general course in literature at university level now that her health would allow it. She was still the most subdued among us. The loss of Em had been harder on Marie than on anybody else.

Yvonne and Cécile had different plans. They were entering the Hôpital Notre Dame de l'Espérance as student nurses. Mom disapproved strongly. They had to contend with her prejudices against anything to do with the medical profession. But they were not to be argued out of this choice. So, although Mom would have been far happier to see us back in Nicolet for another year, it was reluctantly agreed that we might all go to Montreal.

For Yvonne and Cécile to train as nurses was no lightly conceived ambition for either of them. The idea had been turned over in their minds for a long time. As the differences in personality between us grew more and more sharply defined, the two of them emerged as the strong-willed, the less dominated, the more inclined to speak up freely. They shared a room in the nurses' quarters at the rear of the sprawling old buildings in Côte Vertu, a suburb of Montreal to the north of the city, from whose streets may be seen the panorama of the St. Lawrence and the countryside beyond. The corridors of the hospital bore the perpetual faint odor of antiseptics

164

and anesthetics that no nurse ever forgets, but for the two of them it was the sweet smell of freedom.

This was completely unlike the Institut at Nicolet. Here they had as much privacy as they desired, locks on doors, a room of their own to study in. For any student nurse, work is often hard, but perhaps they found it harder than most, because they lagged behind in general education. On top of anatomy and physiology and the rest of the curriculum, they had a lot of catching up to do. And they were painfully shy. But they were in the constant, carefree company of other students, outsiders who were far from being strangers, because they met at most hours of the day, girls on every side to talk to and, very timidly, to get to know as friends. Instead of finding make-up forbidden, as it had been at Nicolet, the order here was that a young nurse should wear a touch of lipstick to brighten up the patients' spirits. Putting on that lipstick every morning was another milestone passed.

The College Marguerite Bourgeois, which stands on a hilltop in Westmount overlooking a seemingly endless expanse of trees and roof tops, was no more than four miles away. There Annette and Marie moved into next-door rooms to the rear of the main block of classrooms. Their reactions to their new surroundings were very much the same as those of Yvonne and Cécile, which is probably not surprising. The atmosphere lacked the scent of antiseptics, but it bore the same fragrance of freedom, and the nuns of Les Dames de la Congregation, who conduct the college, added a fair share of hard work.

Living two by two and apart from each other, each pair of us was often lonesome for the other half of our quartet. We always were when we were apart for more than a day or so at a time, and we always shall be, without any doubt. The feeling is as deep as thirst or hunger, but it is difficult to put into words. Possibly a bird ex-

165

periences the same sensation before it migrates, or an animal when it sniffs water in the distance somewhere. Each of us has it, though not in exactly the same degree at the same time. It is a kind of pull, an attraction that obliterates distance or immediate circumstances. A longing develops to see the others, or if not to see, then at least to write or receive a letter or a telephone call. Unhappiness comes if we stay too long apart and isolated. That was one of the important lessons we learned in the first months in Montreal.

There was much journeying to and fro between the hospital and the college. Westmount and Côte Vertu are not especially busy or noisy sections of the city compared with the downtown area and the hustle and bustle of the shops, but we were petrified to venture beyond the grounds of our new homes. To make the journey from the college to the hospital required a bus ride, then a change to another bus, then yet another transfer to a third bus line. We regarded buses with grave suspicion, as an undependable and dangerous means of transportation, so we invariably covered the four miles by cab. The fares made a big hole in our spending money, which continued to be doled out by Dad and accounted for by him every month to Percy Wilson.

We read somewhere that Em's share of Quintuplet funds amounted to $171,035. It was to be divided into equal parts between Mom, Dad, our seven other sisters and brothers, and ourselves. But the figure had no meaning when we were used only to seeing a few dollars at a time. We had no experience in handling money in larger sums than that, though our twenty-first birthday was drawing close. Nothing had changed in that respect after our flight to Montreal.

Mom constantly questioned our spending habits. "You are so extravagant," she said when one of us splurged on a brassiere. The sight of a ring displayed on a counter in Woolworth's once captivated Annette, and she bought the bit of costume jewelry on her charge account. Then, remorseful and frightened at what would surely be said at home when the bill arrived, she tried to persuade the salesgirl to alter the figure on the slip. The ring had cost one dollar.

The allowances we received were not entirely ours to spend. If we wanted to see a movie in North Bay when we lived in Corbeil, some other members of the family had to go along for security's sake, and we were expected to buy all the tickets. If a package arrived at the Big House when Dad was not there, it was one of us who was expected to pay for it, with little hope of ever being repaid.

This was part and parcel of Mom and Dad's plan to see to it that we were not spoiled or encouraged to think that we were in any way different from the rest. Everyone else, including the family, spoke as though we were privileged and rich, but there was seldom more than a dollar or two in our purses. We grew up with the guilty feeling that somehow we were frittering away money that really belonged to Dad. It was impossible to spend a nickel without wondering if he could afford it.

Because the old links were not completely broken, we sat down dutifully every week in college and hospital to write letters home. From a different sense of duty, on the sixth of each month, the day of her death, we had a Mass said for Em.

We could scarcely have been less prepared to face the ordinary rough-and-tumble of living, even in the simplest things. We were such blushing violets. We did not know how to go out and shop for personal belongings. Nobody had thought fit to show us how to walk into a store, go up to the counter, and exercise a modicum of judgment by choosing a dress. We had no idea what size it should be or how much it ought to cost. If a salesgirl had told any one of us that she needed an eighteen and the price was $1.95, we would have believed her. We had been raised without a shred of independence or mental muscle. We were introverts through and through, imbued with the conviction that we were not capable of making up our own minds about anything or of doing anything without seeking somebody's permission.

We fell into the error of going into downtown Montreal together, the four of us. We felt safer that way. But we were taking too much for granted in the heady days of being free. In a department store, a crowd began to gather around us as though we were a traveling show. Being hemmed in by people, no matter how innocent their curiosity, terrified us. We darted off every which way, like rabbits running for their burrows at the sound of a hunter's gun. The dark glasses we had taken to wearing did not help at all as a disguise.

For long enough after that, we went two by two if we wanted to shop on St. Catherine Street, where the big department stores are to be found—Eaton's, Simpson's, and Henry Morgan's. Then, as furtive as thieves, we would slip in through the revolving doors and pick up almost literally the first blouse or skirt or pair of stockings we could lay hands on, charge it, and make off to the nearest exit. It was more than a year before any one of us dared ask to try on a dress before buying it. The prospect of going into a changing booth for that purpose was inconceivable. What if we were caught in there? Supposing the world, represented in this case by other women out for an hour's shopping, should crowd around the doorway and watch our embarrassment?

Except for underclothes, which remained white and sturdy and exclusively of cotton, our tastes ran invariably to black, usually at least one size too big for us. In street clothes, we probably looked like orphans wearing someone else's castoffs.

168

An infinitely greater problem than learning how to shop or mix with other women was the mystery of men. They represented a riddle that left the mind reeling. We had such mixed emotions that it was not possible to make any sense of them. In our upbringing until this era in Montreal, love and sex had to be regarded as sinful things. That was what we had been led to believe at home, and there had been no change in our attitude at Nicolet. Whereas we knew nothing about money and material things, we existed in a state of abysmal prejudice about the ways of a man with a woman.

In Corbeil, it was looked upon as something close to a sin for a boy to hold a girl's hand, at least until they were engaged, and then it was not to be encouraged. Marriages were made not in Heaven but between the two families involved, more often than not with regard for the dowry the bride-to-be might bring with her, but with little consideration for romantic love. Dad did not approve of our having girl friends, let alone boy friends.

The only members of the male sex that we could talk to without risking his displeasure were neighbors' sons, our brothers, and the admirers, before their marriages, of Thérèse and Rose-Marie who were sometimes allowed into the house to watch a movie or dance to the record player in the basement playroom. Some of the boys on the permissible list struck us as being attractive, but we did not know how to tell them so.

The thrill of holding a boy's hand had happened only once before, a great distance off in time and place. So far as we could detect, we had no need for men's love, because we had never experienced it. There was not the remotest possibility, so we had been taught, of our ever marrying. We were destined to live forever at home or go into the Church as inevitably as water runs down to the sea. We were as weak and as lacking in will power as water is in the matter of changing this destiny. Not the slightest doubt existed in our minds of this.

The guilt we lived with governed our thoughts. Men were not to be loved, but to be distrusted. Happiness was the last thing a woman could anticipate in marriage. And yet it was not quite so simple as that, when we thought about it. Perhaps, we would sometimes fancy, it would be nice to meet a man, someone with an education and kindliness in his manner and goodness in his heart, who would smile and help make the world a friendlier place.

Gradually, in each of our hearts, the spark began to glow, first perhaps in that of Cécile, the most independent of us. We wanted to learn a little about the inscrutable ways of men. This was something else for which we had developed no immunity either. We were ready, eager even, to fall in love with the first presentable candidates who came along.

In Corbeil, one set of barricades was in process of being torn down. The fences around the old nursery were being leveled to the ground. The building itself was inhabited again, and it was in the middle of yet another remodeling. The new tenants were the Recluses of the Order of Jesus and Mary, led by Reverend Mother Rita-Marie. They moved in soon after we left for Montreal.

At first there were just five of them. Their number corresponded with that of the Quintuplets, as the newspapers pointed out after the Reverend Mother gave an interview. Other nuns of the Order would be joining later, she said, so that they could take turns every hour in kneeling and reciting the Rosary perpetually, which would be something new in the predominantly Protestant Province of Ontario.

"The purpose of our community is the perpetual recitation of the Rosary," said the Mother General, "but one of the reasons we decided to establish a monastery here was to memorialize the Quintuplets. Citizens will be welcome to visit."

When they acquired the place from Dad, all the Recluses paid was the token dollar on signature of the agreement, but there turned out to be a hidden flaw in the proceedings. Legally, the nursery belonged to us. The land it stood on had been bought from Dad by the guardians. Together with the buildings put up on that land, the property was listed as an asset worth $60,000. At the time the Recluses took over the nursery, we were under age.

They possessed no money, and they lived from hand to mouth for the six years they maintained the nursery-monastery. Father Armand Aumont, who served as chaplain in the monastery for some two years, was confronted with the perpetual problem of making ends meet. The worry of it must have etched in some of the lines that crisscrossed his gaunt face. His spare frame carried not an ounce of extra flesh. His name is difficult to say in French, so among ourselves we gave him the disrespectful nickname "Father Toothpick" when we set eyes on him for the first time when we went back to the Big House for Christmas. The nuns had converted one room of the former nursery into a tiny chapel, with benches reserved for the Dionnes. We went to midnight Mass there every Sunday and on Christmas Eve.

Father Toothpick and the nuns found any number of ways of eking out a bare living. On the spot where the old observatory had stood before it was demolished and carted away plank by plank to provide building materials for Thérèse's house in Espanola, there were now goats grazing among the grass that had sprung up inches tall. The goats were milked every day, and under one of Father Toothpick's ingenious plans for survival the little herd would have been greatly increased.

171

That would mean taking over the Big House itself, and the chaplain had thought of it, without a doubt, as a means of raising money. Some of the rooms he would convert into a chocolate factory, bringing in the necessary machines and using the milk from the goats. So that no space would be wasted, he had another venture in mind for the cellar. He proposed installing presses, vats and the necessary pipes for making sacramental wine.

He was in deadly earnest about both schemes. He had many informal talks with Dad about buying the house, not at the bargain price for which the nuns had been handed the nursery, but at a realistic figure. That may have been the only realistic aspect of the chaplain's ambitions. In spite of the commercial aspects, the plan was nevertheless conceived, as the Mother General attested, as a memorial to Em and the rest of us.

At the foot of the hill, close to where the goats browsed, the Recluses opened up a souvenir stand of their own to attract the tourist trade. There they sold various souvenirs, each faithfully stamped, "The Recluses of Corbeil." When the appropriate season came around, they offered for sale a line of Christmas cards marked in the same fashion.

But the Mother General's imagination extended far beyond this. It was her dream to have Em taken out of the graveyard and carried into what was now the monastery, her old home. She would be reburied there so that pilgrimages might be made to her tomb. The Mother General asked to do this repeatedly, clearly seeing no harm or hurt to us in her plea and failing to understand why she was always refused.

Accepting the rebuff at last, the Mother General came forward with an alternative proposal. The site which was now the preserve of the goats should be converted into an open-air shrine. Five statues carved in stone of each of us would lead up to a larger one depicting the group of us gathered around the feet of the Virgin.

Nothing came of the idea, just as all the schemes of Father Toothpick and the Mother General were doomed to disappointment in the end. By then, seven gray-garbed nuns worked and prayed at the monastery. The Order made a bid to buy the Big House, at a price of $55,000. Dad wanted an option to repurchase the house if the Recluses ever put it on the market, in order to keep it out of the hands of any religious order but theirs, for which he had a great regard.

The property is owned jointly by the Quintuplets and Em's estate, with Mom and Dad having a life interest in it. He asked for half the total purchase price if it should be sold. There was no assenting to this, and the sale of the Big House was never closed. One day we learned that the Recluses had moved out as inconspicuously as they had moved in. There had been a change of heart, and the Recluses were no longer interested in buying it. They found, too, that the work of caring for the place inside and out, with snow to shovel by the ton every winter, was too much for them to cope with.

The building which had led a checkered career as nursery, school, convent and monastery stood deserted and dark once more. If anything stirred in the rooms where we had once played, it could be only such things as mice, wandering spiders, or the hundred minute creatures that arrive from the fields and woods when human inhabitants depart.

We did not go inside the place. It meant both too much and too little to us.

◄§ TWELVE §►

I T IS NECESSARY to go back in time and place to Montreal and the days shortly after we turned up there to study. There were the customary paragraphs and a few pictures in the papers, some of the facts being reasonably correct, none of the photographs being exceptionally flattering.

One of the stories, in the French-language newspaper *La Patrie*, was read by a young man who had left his home in Quebec City to come down to Montreal and work as a technician in the television studios of the Canadian Broadcasting Corporation. The writer had mentioned that Yvonne and Cécile lived in nurses' quarters at the Hôpital Notre Dame de l'Espérance.

Philippe Langlois, the young man from Quebec City, telephoned there one evening and asked if he could please speak with Cécile. He might easily have asked for any one of us. He chose Cécile, as it turned out later, only because he had a sister with the same name. In any event, Cis was busy at the time, so he left a number and a request that she return his call.

The message that was given her mentioned only the

174

number, no name. Thinking that perhaps a girl friend had been wanting to speak with her, Cécile returned the call. When she found it was a total stranger, and a man at that, who answered, she felt as if she were really on the brink of the breath-taking water of independence. The article in *La Patrie* had reported that we were "sequestered" in Montreal. Cécile was determined to prove that to be an error. She plunged into the ocean, eager to see whether she would sink or swim, by making a date on the telephone to see Philippe Langlois.

To meet a strange man was a test of courage she knew she had to take. If she refused, she would be a coward, she reasoned to herself, unworthy of the new, infinitely more rewarding life we were slowly discovering. Other nurses in training went out on dates. Well then, so would she. When we heard what she had done, we could not have been more astounded if she had announced that she was going to run off with a circus to take a course in taming tigers.

Cécile was the pioneer among us, who dared to explore the unknown and discover what it meant to make a friend from the other half of the human race. Much more than that, she fell in love. From the smile on her lips and the happiness in her eyes, we judged it was good for her and wondered if the same, inexplicable thing might happen to another of us one day.

For the time being, though, Cécile's romance had to be kept a secret among ourselves. Dad certainly could not yet be told about charming, easygoing Philippe, who made Montreal seem many steps closer to paradise when he and she took a walk together or went to a movie or listened to the orchestra that plays outdoors on the heights of Mont Royal every summer.

Not long ago, Philippe said, "I remember very clearly how you looked when we first met. You were wearing a coat at least two sizes too big for you."

"It was black, of course, and reached almost down to my ankles," she agreed. But romance always did ignore such mundane details and perfume the world with roses.

In the surgical ward of the hospital a patient arrived with appendicitis. Gilles Allard came from Drummond-ville, a factory town some sixty miles from Montreal. Yvonne and Cécile knew something of his family. A sister of his, Gertrude, had been employed as cook and cookery teacher at the Villa Notre Dame. A younger sister, also named Cécile, had boarded there as a student. Still another member of this large family, Germain, was living almost around the corner from the hospital, at the Collège of St. Laurent, where he was in his final year as a philosophy student.

Germain came in one day with Gertrude to visit his brother, and that was the start of the discovery by one more of us that men were not always hateful. He was introduced first, by Gertrude, to Cécile and Yvonne. Cécile had come to the conclusion that it was high time for somebody else to begin meeting men. She had a girl in mind for Gerry.

"Annette is studying music at Marguerite Bourgeois," she said. "You should get to know her. How would you like to come and see her some time?"

At the college, a collection of Gothic buildings 150 years old, Gerry had only one free day each month. "Okay," he said. "I shall have a Saturday evening off ten days from now. We will plan to go and see Annette then."

Cécile gave Annette no word about what had been planned, well aware that her sister would have run like a hare at the thought. On the appointed Saturday, Gerry turned up at the college, spic and span, with Cécile, Yvonne, and a new friend they had made among the nurses. They left him alone in the parlor while they went off to trap Annette and send her in.

At the sight of a strange man waiting for her, Annette's instinct was to flee, just as Cécile had anticipated. Covered with confusion, she stood cautiously by the door.

"Are you afraid to be alone with a man?" were the first words that passed between them.

"What do you want me to answer?" she said.

"Would you like to sit down?"

"No, thank you." She would not and could not. She was mad at Cis for putting her in such a predicament. What did one say to a man like this? Besides, a seam in her dress had split open. She dare not sit down in case it showed, and the dress was a workaday thing that she was ashamed of, anyway.

But Cécile's joy with Philippe was contagious and impossible to resist. After their stilted introduction to each other in the parlor, they arranged to meet again. In a little while they exchanged vows of friendship and pictures of each other, each looking very young and very studious. *Fidèle souvenir* was the message written on the back of the photograph Gerry was given.

Most of the time, they spoke English together, as we all did. There was a significance in this. At Dad's insistence, French had been the principal tongue for us through all our school days, and we had been laughed at by the family because our English was not up to their standards of fluency. So, English had become a symbol of the present, a turning away from the past.

The months that followed could not have been so very different from the usual patterns of young people in love, spellbound by romance, which seems to have been invented exclusively for them to make the earth a brand-new and enchanting place in which to live. Only the small, tender details could have been different, the inconsequential things that everyone stores away in memory, to turn over in later years like pages in a book once read and never forgotten.

Until now, we had had so little that any one of us cared to remember. The special miracle was that what was happening now was so completely normal and ordinary, the kind of happiness that average girls enjoyed without brooding over fate or misfortune, only daydreaming of the future and what joy it might bring.

There was an upstairs window where Gerry sat with his books, overlooking the street. On evenings when he could not get out, Cécile and Yvonne would stroll over there and stand below, to gossip and keep him company. There was the Bar-B-Q restaurant where we sometimes ate together, quite an ordinary, inexpensive spot marked by a glittering neon sign, when one sees it today through older eyes. But that too had a part in the magic of those days. We even summoned up the nerve to go there by bus—with two changes on the way—instead of taking a cab, so we were obviously making rapid progress.

It was easy for any newcomer to mistake Cécile and Annette for each other. Both had the same short haircut. Both wore black in memory of Em. Both were perhaps closer in looks than the other two of us. Philippe did not fall into the trap, but Gerry did, with both feet. One Sunday afternoon, he hurried around to the hospital to see the girl he knew would be waiting for him in the downstairs recreation room. They exchanged hellos, then he asked, "How did things go for you in your classes this week?"

"Fine, but the Sisters keep you working very hard, you know."

"When do you take your next exams in music?"

"Oh, at the end of the year. I am so nervous." One of her sisters stood watching the scene from a distance, with arms folded and with fire in her eyes. So it continued, while Gerry showered his companion with con-

178

versation and Cécile mischievously entangled him in her net.

Imagine! Annette was as angry as a hornet. Not with Cécile, for all her tricks, but with Gerry for being incapable of telling her from the other in spite of the love he was always speaking of. When he is in a mood to tease nowadays—and can any husband resist that sometimes?—he is still apt to say, "You know, I'm not sure that I married the right one. Perhaps I should have chosen Cis, after all."

Yvonne and Marie were essential to the fun we were all having, though Marie's part in it was quieter. She was not to be allowed to find life so pleasant much longer. At that time, she was more reserved, more introspective than the others. The loss of Em still weighed heavily on her, and she badly needed the spark of happiness.

Marie is the one with the greatest sense of pity, the one whose heart is most readily moved. Toward the end of November, a little more than two months after our arrival in Montreal, she went home for a weekend. She did not come back. Mom and Dad had not yielded in their opposition to our being away from them. Though they knew nothing of Gerry and Phil, they were offended and outraged that we had left the Big House for lives of our own.

On the first day of December, Dad had one of his announcements to make to *The Nugget* and the news agencies: Marie had quit college and returned home. "She simply didn't like what she was doing," he said, "and both her mother and I are very glad to have one of the Quints home with us." We could reach our own conclusions about his choice of words.

A knowing reporter found that her decision was not in the least surprising, since "people who knew the girls well" were aware that Marie got "real satisfaction and enjoyment in helping her mother around the house."

Unhappily, none of that was true. When Marie arrived for that momentous weekend, Mom broke out with a stream of complaints about feeling lonely without us, though she was by no means deserted. Ernest and his family lived a stone's throw away in the old staff house. Victor and Claude still remained under the same roof as Mom and Dad. "I want you to stay here with me," she told Marie tearfully, and Mom would sometimes use tears as an argument.

There and then, Marie abandoned her plan to go back to college when her weekend was over. She had left Montreal with every intention of returning, but she could not bring herself to leave Mom in such a state of misery. We did not see Marie again until Christmas came around, and we all went up to Corbeil for the holidays.

Marie had fallen back into the old pattern. She had little choice but to take on the burden of housework again. There were no other girls at home to help, and the house had certainly grown no smaller in our absence. In fact, with more of the rooms empty, it appeared to be bigger and less intimate than before. The family looked us over in the course of conversation and let us know that we had changed for the worse since we had been away. As soon as Christmas was over, it was a relief to leave again. It had not been a happy visit for anyone. The only sorrow we felt at leaving was that Marie was not coming with us.

From Dad's point of view, the year that lay ahead was possibly the most important of our lives. Next May, we should be twenty-one and totally independent in the eyes of the law. On that date, according to the Guardianship Act, the inheritance and the properties which had been held in our name were to be handed over to us. Dad's day as comptroller of the purse strings was rapidly coming to an end. As ever, he went to great pains to try to shape events as he wanted them, to make the future conform to his way of thinking.

He always had the rare ability to fix his mind on a target and keep it there, much as a ship's captain charts a course for a far-off shore. What Dad said or did at any single time might not appear on the face of it to have anything to do with his long-range plan, but one could be sure that, like a ship changing course for reasons of weather, he was making for a home port somewhere.

At least five years earlier, he had begun putting abroad the idea that we ought to invite him to continue his reign over the money. When we were sixteen, he inspired a friendly writer to ask in print if we would retain Dad, who "keeps track of every dollar that is spent," as a business manager—because "they couldn't get a better one."

He enlisted the movies as a means of educating us in the importance of having money wisely looked after. He insisted that we see *The Heiress*, as portrayed by Olivia de Havilland, who was wooed, and made miserable, by Montgomery Clift. From this, Dad underlined the moral: rich girls must beware of fortune hunters.

As the momentous birthday drew nearer, he tackled the subject from yet another angle. We were away in Montreal when he had a dependable reporter in for an interview in the study of the Big House.

"In my desk there," he declared, pointing across the room, "I have many letters asking for the girls to make public appearances. One offered me twenty thousand dollars a week, just for their appearance. But we have consistently refused to let them be made into side-show freaks. The publicity has been bad enough. It would have been easy, with all the adulation, for the Quints to get to thinking they were better than other people." There were concealed meanings in his words once more.

181

Only the family could correctly interpret what he was saying about us.

One month before the red letter day on our calendars, he invited Mort Fellman in for another long talk, which *The Nugget* was happy to report on its front page. "Four Quints To Receive $800,000 Next Month," the headline said. "There is a strong likelihood that the Quints will decide to set up their own trust fund when the Supreme Court of Ontario turns it over to them on their twenty-first birthday," wrote Mr. Fellman. "They have indicated that they have something like this in mind, and Lawyer Donnelly is now working on such a plan for their consideration." Dad's view was made plain. He was quoted as telling the editor, "I don't think that coming into the money is going to make any difference at all."

Now he was not avoiding reporters but making himself available to them in order that there should be no doubt about his position. He told another caller from the press that from now on we were welcome to Dad's advice or help. "But when I was twenty-one I didn't lean on my parents much. Maybe we'll give them money for their birthday." He said, and it was easy for anyone to believe him, "I've always done my best for them. I wonder how many people realize that. Not many, I guess. All we want is for them to be happy."

Like the famous American comedian, Will Rogers, we sometimes learned everything we knew from the newspapers, but we did not regularly see *The Nugget* in Montreal. We often fell behind in our knowledge of what Dad had been saying, since he would speak more freely to the newspapers than to us.

Trust agreements were actually being drawn up in law offices in North Bay—four agreements, one for each of us to sign—but we were unaware of it. Dad was so eager to have us accept them as they stood that he told the

182

newspapers we had put our signatures to these documents when we had not even had a chance to inspect them.

The original plan was for Mom to come to Montreal for the birthday celebration, to give her a holiday, too, and a chance to see something of the city to which she was a stranger. Then, unexpectedly, Annette, Cécile, and Yvonne were summoned up to Corbeil. Mom would not be coming down, and there was important business to attend to up there.

We went up on the early train. No special plans for the celebration had been disturbed, because we had planned no big party. Such things were not for us. The atmosphere in the Big House was all business, little festivity. Mom had baked a birthday cake for each of the four of us, complaining to herself as she worked in the kitchen that really one cake ought to do and having five birthdays on a single day had always been a terrible inconvenience for everybody.

The four of us were asked into the library for a ceremonious reading of the trust agreements. Each was exactly the same document with only the name differing. We were completely in the dark about what to expect. Dad had never discussed business like this with us. But we held no great hope that this time anything pleasant might happen. It would have been too much to expect. In the paneled room with its yellow ceiling and massive chandelier, Dad was waiting with Lawyer Donnelly. Also there was a man from the Guaranty Trust Company, which had always had custody of the money, and a second attorney, whom we had not seen before. It was he who read aloud the eight typewritten pages of the agreement. He went through it just once, in English, then Dad asked us to sign. We had picked up only a hint of what the involved legal phrases meant.

"May we hear it again?" asked Cécile.

So the attorney read through the "whereases" and "heretofores" and "settlors" once again. Now then surely, Dad said, we were prepared to sign.

We stood in silence for a moment, then turned to each other. There was no mistaking the significance of it. Everyone in the room must have sensed it. Two points of view, Dad's and ours, were in violent collision, and somehow the silence only made it worse. Who would be the first with the courage to say it?

"No," said Cécile firmly and clearly. "It is impossible to sign without a chance to study it first." We nodded our heads quickly in agreement with her. With outsiders there, Dad could not make a scene or argue. It was accepted that signing would have to wait until another day. We sat down briefly to slice the birthday cakes, then caught the afternoon train back to Montreal, each with eight intimidating pages of homework to pore over.

Once signed, each document was "irrevocable"; it said so plainly enough. It gave the "settlor," meaning ourselves, control of all the income from the trust but not of the principal sum. That was to be ours, for the most part, in three installments, payable at the age of thirty-one, thirty-nine, and forty-five. The last payment would leave about one third of the capital intact and untouchable, to be shared among any children we might have or, if there were none, among the Dionne family. If any of us died unmarried, her estate went first to Mom and Dad, then had to be passed on in equal shares to each brother and sister. The Big House and the land on which it stood were to remain subject to Mom's and Dad's right to "enjoy and occupy" during their lifetimes.

In some ways, the agreements had the effect of a will. They reached out over the generation after our own. Before we signed, we should seek the advice of someone we could rely on for an objective and independent opinion,

184

somebody who would not be tempted to influence us in one direction or another.

One of us went to see the priest of our Westmount parish and took along the agreement for him to read. In his opinion, there was nothing to object to in the provisions set forth paragraph by paragraph, but we remained doubtful. We could not trust what we could not entirely understand, and that line about "irrevocable" made us think twice and more. The days slipped by, and still the agreements were not signed. We heard nothing from home.

One week later, Yvonne was on duty at the hospital, Cécile had the day off, and she and Annette wanted to ride out to Nicolet to visit a friend of ours who lived in the town. Gerry was invited along for the trip, and he needed no urging to accept. None of us had a car, so a taxi was the simplest means of getting there. Cécile rode with the driver, Annette and Gerry in the back. The three of them had been asked to dinner at the home of Gertrude Lupien, whom we had met in college. It was a happy family, the Lupiens, and the whole house was shaking with laughter within minutes of arrival.

The fun was at its peak when the telephone rang. A call from the Institut Familial. Mom had arrived in Nicolet, too, and she was looking for us. Ernest had driven her from Corbeil with Marie, who had come to the conclusion that the least painful escape from the Big House, least difficult for everyone concerned, would be for her to enroll for a summer course at the Institut. On their road to Nicolet, they had stopped in Montreal, at the hospital, where Yvonne had told them that, by chance, Cécile and Annette were already in the town they were headed for.

After the telephone call to the Lupiens, Cécile and Annette promised to meet Mom in one of the town's restaurants for a cup of coffee together. She could have made the journey for only one purpose, so far as they could judge. She had come to argue about the trust agreements. Mom was unaware that Gerry existed, and this was obviously no time for her to learn about him. It was best for him to stay behind at the Lupiens' when the two girls left and make his own way home alone by bus.

Ernest's car was parked outside the restaurant. Marie sat in it, not saying a word beyond a subdued hello. Inside the restaurant, Mom was in a mood of great distress.

"Why won't you sign?" she asked. "You will lose a lot of money if you are so stubborn. Please sign for your own sakes as well as for ours." The two of them began to waver. "Dad is so upset," Mom went on. "He is really sick because of the delay. Why don't you sign?"

It was impossible to resist forever. "Very well," Cécile said. "I will do it." Annette agreed that there was no alternative. Marie, with none of us to discuss the business with in Corbeil, had yielded earlier. Her signature was already on paper.

After Marie had been delivered to the college, Ernest took Mom back with Annette and Cécile to Montreal. We had the draft agreements there. The party of them got back toward the end of that evening. It was a strange setting that was found for the formal but simple act that signified our financial independence. At the rear of the hospital, under the trees outside the nurses' quarters, in the slowly fading light, Yvonne, Cécile, and Annette put their names to the trust agreements; they used the trunk of Ernest's car as a desk. As a set of four, the documents governed the future disposition of close to one million dollars.

When our brother had driven Mom away, the reaction set in. It had been a tense, disturbing day. We felt, rightly or wrongly, that we had been treated unfairly,

186

persuaded with arguments having little to do with the issue involved, and we were sick at heart about it. We had a long way to go before we could match our wits or our will power with Dad's. He remained the master within the family.

◦§ THIRTEEN §◦

A**T FIRST** it looked as though Dad was right in what
he had said and it did make no difference whatever
whether or not we controlled our own money and our
own method of life. True enough, we could have been
immediately much better off financially if we took up
the proposal of the Guaranty Trust Company, which
would pay us a hundred dollars a month each. But we
were not used to such wealth. We could see no need for
it, so we would have thought ourselves greedy to accept.
We said no, we wanted only half that amount.

In theory, we were free as birds; yet old, ingrained
habits die exceedingly hard. One by one, the threads that
bound us to past pleasures and past pain were being
snapped. But we shaped our ways by the memory of the
conditions that had existed until only a few months ago.
We were secretive about ourselves. We were scared half
to death of more hounding by reporters and cameramen,
so we let very few people know anything of where we
lived and in what manner. We were unwilling to confide
much in Mom or Dad, especially any hint about Phil or
Gerry.

At the hospital, Yvonne was evidently destined to be a dedicated nurse. She asked for little more than the immense satisfaction of serving the sick, most of all in the children's wards, and in observing the colors and shapes of the world for interpretation in her painting. There were those who said she probably had more than an amateur's talents.

Most of Cécile's off-duty hours were shared with Phil. A student nurse has little time to herself, but what there was they spent together. They went to concerts. They took in movies by the dozen so that she might understand in rapid order something of the realities we had been missing. They did Cécile's shopping for new clothes together, with Phil gradually changing her tastes and delighting in seeing her in less somber colors—and sizes that fit. If the universe could have stopped revolving then and those days have gone on forever, she would not have objected.

Marie was experiencing the hardest time in emerging from the cocoon. Her spirit was eager, but she had to marshal her strength. She had not yet had enough time to begin to find herself as the rest of us were doing. After the summer at Nicolet, she believed she would be strong enough to stand up to convent discipline again. That beckoning alternative continued to influence the majority of us. Only Cécile by now had made up her mind that she wanted marriage, not the veil of a nun.

Without going back to Corbeil, Marie left Nicolet and returned to the convent of the Servants of the Very Holy Sacrament in Quebec City. The authorities there accepted her as a novice, not a postulant, which would have been the usual thing. She was allowed to take up where she had left off a year earlier, wearing white, not a newcomer's black. Because she had not formally left the order, the parchment with its promise to obey God, which she had signed on the altar with the other postulants, had been kept in the convent. She was bound by it to return to the life of the cloister.

This was a time of profound stirring, of self-searching, of adjustment. Cécile and Yvonne had crowded days and nights with textbooks to study as well as patients to nurse in the wards. Annette, in a sense, was the uncommitted one. Only she had the time, or the desire, to go home that first summer of being adult.

She took the train alone to North Bay, then a taxi from the station. She let herself in through the gates of the Big House and walked slowly up the asphalt driveway. The front lawn was deserted. Not a sound came from the house. The whole countryside seemed asleep. A chill ran through her as a memory of everything that the house stood for suddenly entered her mind. Outside the side door that opened straight into the kitchen she stood undecided while one minute followed another. She asked herself over and over again whether it would be best to turn her back and catch the train again without even going in to say hello. But old habits are strong. She took a deep breath and opened the kitchen door.

She spent a strange summer, alone with herself among the remainder of the family, conscious more sharply of the need to be with one of her own kind, one of us. As often as possible, she worked outdoors, where human problems were diminished by the majesty of the earth itself. She spoke to Mom and Dad only of mundane things—the weather, the minor events of each day—and kept silent about Gerry. She spent hours at the cemetery in the farmer's field, cleaning up Em's grave. The grass had been allowed to grow up tall round it. There was no trace of a flower. The little wire fence that had been put around after the funeral had been removed. That was Mom's wish. She may have thought of it as a different kind of barrier separating a Quintuplet from those of her forebears. To satisfy Mom, another fence had been erected that included the ground where our grandparents lay. Cows wandered around the headstones beyond the new barrier.

The summer passed in a kind of dream. Free will had disappeared once again, and only fate controlled the future. Annette decided then that music, which had been a special delight of hers, would not serve as a career for her. Did she want to allow herself to fall in love? She did not know. But if she wanted something different, she would have to train for it. What was it that she would like most of all to make of herself? The answer was sometimes almost within her grasp.

Perhaps she should follow the example of Cécile and Yvonne and work to be a nurse. That was what she set her mind to, but Mom was not in favor. Mom argued so passionately against the mere suggestion that Annette did not oppose her. Two nurses among us were more than enough, Mom thought, because the medical profession had not managed to restore itself in her estimation. One could not tell her that her suspicions about the mischief that went on between doctors and nurses were not to be taken as the truth.

We were so ignorant for so long about how many choices were open to us, and to anyone with the wish to explore them. So few doors seemed to stand open for us to enter, and each of them had to be reassuringly familiar or we were afraid to make the effort. Annette applied to re-enter Nicolet, which was territory well-trodden and therefore almost friendly. She chose different courses this time. One was teaching. Another was psychology, which from the first classes she attended held a fascination for her.

The quiet days at the Institut Familial did not last very long. They came to an end literally in an avalanche. On the morning of Saturday, November 12, a letter was delivered to her from the Mother Superior of the convent of the Servants of the Very Holy Sacrament. Marie, it said, had fallen ill again.

Annette's thought was to go to Quebec City as soon as she could, that weekend. It did not appear to be an urgent matter, so she was content to wait without asking to leave early. At eleven o'clock, she was down in the basement of the Institut's dormitory building, killing time by tidying up her locker.

Suddenly, the earth itself roared, and the whole town threatened to disappear. She was certain that the straining walls around her would collapse, as the sound of chaos increased, and she would be killed before the next breath. She was only one of thousands terrorized by the din of destruction. The question flashed across her brain, to be dismissed in a split second's reflection, that if she died then, she would not care too much. She raced upstairs.

The college was a mad place of white-faced nuns and screaming girls. Outside, the streets looked like a wartime city after an enemy bombardment, with rubble piled high where buildings had stood only minutes before. Dust shrouded everything, and flames were flickering in the ruins.

For twenty-five years, there had been clear signs that the steep clay banks of the River Nicolet were being undermined by the flow of water. Nothing had been done about it, either by the town or by the province. Now the land had fallen away and swallowed up a full third of the town. A hole seventy feet deep and an acre across marked the heart of the devastation.

Complete buildings had gone down brick by brick into the river. The boys' school run by the Christian Brothers had vanished, along with an apartment house and a gas station. The bridge was wrecked. Telephone poles had been snapped like toothpicks. The Cathedral of St. Jean Baptiste was damaged beyond repair. In his palace,

Archbishop Albertus Martin had been pacing slowly along a cloister, reading his breviary, when stone blocks and timbers crashed behind him. He bolted to safety. Out in the street, one could see what remained of the palace, sliced neatly in two and opened to the sky like a doll's house.

Running into the street, Annette saw panic everywhere. People darted aimlessly into their houses and out again, up the streets, then back, petrified lest the land would heave again and finish off everything and everybody. Already a thousand souls were homeless. Later it was learned that a doctor's child had been lost when the house was dashed into the river. The cook at the Christian Brothers' school had been killed in the ruins, and so had a lay brother. She had died trying to save him. On any other day but Saturday, three hundred boys would have been at their lessons when the walls about them came thundering down.

Evacuation of the town was the only possible course. The fires were spreading uncontrolled out of the wreckage. Fire engines, police cars and army trucks brought in men to fight the flames. Patients were carried on stretchers out of the hospital and loaded into hastily summoned ambulances. The convent was emptied by order of the authorities.

In this world turned upside down, Annette did not know where to turn, only that somehow she should go to Quebec City to see Marie. She managed to reach Gertrude Lupien by telephone, hoping that she could seek refuge there. But the Lupien house was in a forbidden zone. Town officials had decreed that it was too dangerous for anyone to go there, because it was likely that the land would cascade into the water.

So Annette decided she could go only to Gerry; we were always so short of friends to turn to. Before she set off, she made the rounds of her classmates, who were scattered in the town, collecting telephone numbers of their families and friends so that she might tell them the girls were safe, even though much of the town was in ruins. Then she picked her way to the main highway, to hitchhike to Gerry's home in Drummondville.

"My aunt opened the door when you knocked, as I remember well," Gerry said recently. "You arrived at suppertime. You could not have realized how you looked —tired out, stunned, covered in dust."

He was home for the weekend from the university. He had heard on the radio about the avalanche, and he was chewing his fingernails with anxiety. At the Allards', Annette sat down and wrote a letter to Dad and Mom to tell them she had escaped unscathed and was in Drummondville "at the house of a friend." The letter went unanswered.

Gerry's name, or the name of his family, was still not to be mentioned for fear of the storm that might break if Dad caught on to the fact that there were boy friends in the picture. A friend of Gerry's drove him and Annette to Montreal, where she made the promised telephone calls to the names on her list, passing on the news that her classmates were alive. She spent the night with Yvonne and Cécile in the nurses' quarters at the hospital, then caught an afternoon train to Quebec City and Marie.

Marie had been taken into a hospital, the Hôtel Dieu. It was Annette's task to deliver a message she had been given by the Mother Superior of the convent: Marie could not be taken back when she left this sickbed. The general state of her health combined with the acute loneliness she endured would not permit her to continue. She would have to surrender her desire to become a nun. Annette found her lying in bed, wearing starched coif and serge habit, as required by the rules of the order even in illness. It was difficult to tell, and more difficult to hear, that the Church could not be her chosen life. Of necessity, she would have to seek some other road to contentment, if that were possible.

They went back to Montreal by taxi, stopping off at the convent only to pick up Marie's clothes and the few possessions which had been stored away since her return. Her vows were automatically canceled and control of her inheritance was returned.

Any kind of situation, no matter how challenging, was much easier to handle now that we had trust agreement money of our own to spend, with nobody peering over our shoulders and questioning the fate of every dollar. Annette and Marie rented a furnished apartment on Côte St.-Luc, in a new building on a street where several similar blocks stood, at two hundred dollars a month.

So yet another page was turned. They could sample living in an apartment house, with all its advantages in convenience and accessibility to the city, and all its noise and confinement. They were learning very fast, it seemed, and the pace often left them distinctly bewildered.

The apartment was a happy enough place. They lived comfortably there, cooking for each other, sleeping late if they felt like it, and they often did, giving a small party for a few close friends now and then, learning something of social life in a busy metropolis, where everything was so utterly different from what we had been used to. For the sake of privacy, they had their telephone listed in the name of another nurse, and the newspapers were fooled for the time being.

They had room enough to sleep four if necessary. That made it simple for Cécile and Yvonne to look after Marie when Netta returned to Nicolet two weeks later. The broken town had only just begun the task of putting itself together again. Evidence of its ordeal could be seen on every side, in the piles of debris, the damaged buildings, the streets, which were no longer thoroughfares but dead ends, interrupted by the gigantic cave-in. The Institut was scarcely half full. The parents of the other girls had decided it was not safe to let them return.

For us all, the apartment in Montreal was a kind of sanctuary, the first home we had shared as adults. It was usually crowded with clothes, the records we liked to dance to, books and magazines to read, the thousand scattered belongings of four women whose work was cut out to keep the place halfway tidy. They were good days, but they did not last very long.

Christmas, only a few weeks ahead, brought trouble, some scandalous headlines, and a wide-open rift in the family that set tongues talking everywhere. Seen in perspective, it was no more than a storm in a teacup, inevitable possibly when Mom and Dad had to learn how to get along without us and we without them. But at the time it seemed like a hurricane.

Work at the hospital kept Cécile and Yvonne forever busy. The days slipped by faster than ever before. They would climb into bed too weary sometimes to take care of anything but the necessities of existence, with no time to spare for social graces. It is apparently not an uncommon situation for student nurses. Marie and Annette had both entered the hospital as patients, one with anemia, the other with a suspected back injury, which proved to be nothing of consequence.

As a result of two being short of time and the other two limited in their opportunity, our Christmas card, signed by all, to Mom and Dad did not go into the mail until December 22. We hoped to spend the holiday together in our delightful new hideaway, quietly and peacefully and restfully, doing very little but enjoying the chance to see one another without interruption for a day or so. Cécile and Yvonne needed the break in their routine. Annette and Marie were not discharged from the hospital until Christmas Eve.

One corner of the veil of secrecy with which we hid ourselves had been lifted. Mom had entered the hospital as a patient, too, a little while earlier, needing treatment for trouble with her legs. She had been introduced to Gerry and at least she had not shown open dislike of him. She was not supposed to mention Gerry to Dad when she got home, but in all probability she did—it was expecting too much for her to withhold such intriguing news from him. Phil's existence, however, was still unrevealed.

In Corbeil, Dad could count on receiving telephone calls from the newspapers every May 28 and at Christmastime, asking how the Quintuplets were spending the birthday and holiday, year after year. But this time he was asked questions that he could not answer. He was uncertain where we would be or what he could say about us. We had not known ourselves whether Marie and Annette would be out of the hospital for Christmas Day, so it had been impossible to give him information in advance.

He must have grown tired of fending off reporters' questions. He may have been prompted by someone in the family. Perhaps he wanted to anticipate the inevitable changes in relationships between us now that we were grown up and the legends that he had constructed so carefully for twenty-one years were bound to be exposed.

Two days after Christmas, he spoke about us to the *Toronto Star*, the paper that he formerly had no use for. We had sent no cards and made no telephone call to him or the family, he said. "We were not surprised when the Quints did not come home for Christmas. We have realized for some months that they have been drifting away from us. Both Mrs. Dionne and I blame outsiders for this separation." He declared that he knew who these

197

"outsiders" were, but he was prepared to say no more about them.

"The Quints lately have been treating their brothers and sisters almost with contempt. A lot of people have asked me why the girls are not home for Christmas. They find it strange, and I don't blame them. Mrs. Dionne and I have given this thing a lot of thought, and we decided it would be best if we didn't try to camouflage things any longer. We have seen it growing for a long time now." He concluded bitterly, "We suspected that outsiders were trying to influence the Quints some years ago, and we were sure of it by the way they acted toward us after they left home, and then more so when they reached their twenty-first birthday and came into their money."

The meaning of it all, every word of his outburst, was clear enough to us when we heard what he had said. His feelings could be explained only in terms of what had gone before. He could not bear to let us go. He had fought tooth and nail to prevent it. He wanted to keep us for himself alone. The moments of victory had been sweet when he had won us back from the combination of forces that had originally taken us away—the doctor, the government, the guardians—and that victory should have lasted perpetually, to please Dad. If he had his way, the walls would always have stood unscalable, retaining us behind them, isolated from life.

The talk of "outsiders" was all too familiar. The "outsiders" he blamed in the past were the priests and nuns who had instructed us and opened our eyes, however slightly, to other things beyond Corbeil and family pride and jealousy. The "outsiders" now were the few friends, men and women, that we were making for the first time in our new circumstances.

As soon as the interview reached the newspapers, reporters set out to hunt us down. The pressure was on again now for them to find us in spite of our precautions. Perhaps they were given a clue at the hospital. It does not matter now. Anyway, the doorbell of the apartment rang. Another nurse, who was visiting with us, answered. A gentleman of the press thrust his foot in the door while she tried to close it and he shouted questions at us. Another of them, after quizzing the superintendent of the building, immediately rented an empty apartment overlooking ours, so that he could watch us through the windows.

None of us wanted to say a word in public. After the tumult in Corbeil, we hoped that silence might have the effect of pouring oil on these troubled seas. It was a vain hope. When a story like this could be built up into more and more headlines, we were probably foolish to believe that we could lie low and escape the hunters' attentions.

Reporters soon tracked Yvonne to the hospital and cornered her there. What had she to say about the Christmas card crisis? She answered briefly through tears. "Don't believe it. It is not true. We sent a card. Is it our fault if they did not get it?" It must be said that the missing card did finally turn up in Corbeil as evidence in our favor.

A cordon of reporters was now besieging the apartment. Phil managed to slip in by the back way, bringing the newspapers in which the Dionnes were creating such a disturbance, together with a few groceries. As soon as we saw the headlines, we realized that this was no small affair in which we were involved. Silence simply was not a sufficient response. For everyone's sake, we had to go to Corbeil, come what may, for a fair talk with Dad. Peace had to be restored somehow. Cécile telephoned Gerry to ask him to accompany us for moral support. If we were going to face Dad, we needed a dependable "outsider" on our side.

Nobody was being excluded from the turmoil. Every

discoverable member of the family had been tracked down for questioning, including Oliva, who was serving in the Royal Canadian Air Force and was stationed at St. Hubert, five miles or so southeast of Montreal. He and a friend had some leave due to them. Oliva agreed to drive us, along with his companion, to Corbeil. Somehow we had to escape unseen from the apartment. We must have made a dozen different plans before we hit on something that had a slim chance of working.

Oliva, his friend and Gerry were to wait for us at the home of Larry Edwards, the branch manager of the Guaranty Trust Company, with whom we were well acquainted; he had agreed on the telephone to be our ally in this venture. The superintendent of the apartment building came up with the idea of smuggling Annette, Yvonne and Cécile down in the service elevator to the basement and through to the garage, where his car would be parked. Marie would stay behind, not yet well enough to endure the long drive, with one of the girls from the hospital for company.

It was ten o'clock on a bitterly cold December night before the last details had been agreed. We hurried out of our front door to the elevator, then down without a stop. The garage was pitch black—the superintendent was not going to provide any clues that we were making our getaway. Feeling our way between the rows of cars, we crept to his, climbed into the back seat and carefully arranged ourselves on the floor, out of sight, clutching the packages we were taking to the family. He started the motor. Squeezed in together like children in a party game, we suspected that at any second we should be discovered. But nothing went astray. Undetected, he left the garage. The streets were inches deep in snow, a typical Montreal winter, when month after month of bitter weather piles up rafted ice ten feet thick and more on the St. Lawrence. Yet, outside the apartment house, shivering reporters were mounting guard. It must be confessed that we had very little pity to spare for them.

We reached the home of Larry Edwards safely and unseen. But the persistent men who cover the news had foreseen that we might turn in this direction. More reporters were stationed outside there. They undoubtedly saw us scurry out of the car and in through the front door for a hasty farewell drink. Fortunately, the rear door provided an unnoticed means of escape. A few feet from it, in one of the narrow alleys which are common in much of Montreal, Oliva was waiting in his car. We had time to load the presents we were taking home into the trunk before we crowded into the rear seat.

A grisly mixture of snow and sleet was beginning to cover the streets with new layers of white. The plan was to drive all night so that we would reach Corbeil before morning. We set out for Highway 17, wheels slithering, windshield wipers clicking monotonously, heater whirring to keep out the cold.

At Petawawa, Ontario, about halfway on our journey, we stopped at an all-night service station for gas and some coffee. We were congratulating ourselves on the success of our ruse, but we thought it best to stay out of sight in the car. Gerry and Oliva went into the little restaurant to buy the coffee for us. Just inside the door, good luck turned to bad. By sheer chance, they almost bumped into Phyllis Griffiths, a reporter for the *Toronto Telegram* and one of our most determined pursuers over the course of many a year. She had hired a car and driver to take her and a photographer from Montreal to Corbeil. Like us, they had stopped for coffee and gas. If we had arrived one minute later, our paths would not have crossed quite like this.

One look at Oliva and she hurried out the door over to the car, where we sat hunched down in our topcoats. She put her head in through the window and began firing questions at us, which we answered in monosyllables. Then she had the cameraman snap a fast flashlight picture, also through the window, which left us blinking like owls. Without wasting a moment, the two of them got into her hired car and sped off down the highway, to beat us to the Big House.

It was 4 A.M. when we reached there. The temperature had fallen to several degrees below zero. The whole scene looked no more hospitable than the South Pole, but a guard of gentlemen from the press, not excluding Miss Griffiths, was braving frostbite to cluster around the entrance gates. No matter how they stamped their feet and beat their arms against themselves, it was a wonder how they could survive until morning.

At the sight of this frozen little army, Oliva did not pause, but instead drove straight on down the road to Callander. From a gas station there, he telephoned Dad. New strategy had to be devised to get us into the house without being surrounded.

It was proposed that Maurice Girouard, who was visiting the house with Rose-Marie, would wait just inside the closed gates until the car came in sight. Then he would open up for a moment to let us through, locking up immediately we were in. Oliva turned back to Corbeil. When he reached the gates, our nerve failed and we begged him to keep going. He granted us a few minutes more, then approached the house a second time. Again we pleaded with him for a little longer, so that we might summon up the courage we so sadly lacked, and again he listened to us. On the third try, Maurice let us through, and we whipped up the driveway in a cloud of spun snow.

We were so scared that we half hoped there would be an accident, a skid, anything that would put us into hospital so we could avoid confronting Dad. Flash bulbs

202

flared on the other side of the gates as we entered the house, but the reporters had no chance to tackle us.

We were tense and shaken, weary after more than eight hours on the road, and dreading this meeting. The family was awake and waiting up for us. Annette made the opening move. She led Gerry over to introduce him to Dad.

"Je te présente Germain," she said, the words falling over her tongue. It was not a good beginning. We had always been taught to address Dad, in French, with the formal *vous*, never the more familiar *tu*. In her nervousness, she had forgotten.

Dad frowned. "What did you say to me?" The atmosphere was as cold as the darkness outside. Annette made a hurried apology and went through the introduction once more. For half an hour, we sat around and spoke in generalities, about the weather, our health and theirs, anything but the purpose of our expedition. A little of the chill was taken off the conversation by our going into the *salon de cuir* to present belated Christmas gifts we had brought loaded in the trunk. At long last, we went upstairs to snatch a few hours' sleep, with nothing said on either side about the crisis within the family. Dad would choose his own time.

Throughout the day that followed, the same rules prevailed, as if this were just another visit that would end with the usual *au revoir*, and we were in our teens again, home for the holidays from boarding school. The newspapers had it that we had all been served a turkey dinner to celebrate the patching up of the public squabble. In fact, we sat down that day around the great dining room table, covered in oil cloth, and Mom served spaghetti.

Before supper, Dad asked us to go with him into the library. Mom was not invited, and Gerry was excluded as a stranger. Once the door was closed, no more time was wasted. It was not Dad who set the ball rolling.

Cécile spoke up for all of us. She was truly angry. "Why did you talk to the newspapers and start all this?" she demanded. "What made you tell these things about us? Why did you make trouble when we have never said a word about anything?"

For once, Dad did not attempt to blame us or berate us. All the evidence was on our side. He accepted what we told him, admitted that he had erred in talking for publication and stirring up the crisis, ostensibly over no more than a missing Christmas card.

"All the talking was done by you," we lectured him. "We could have said much more, you know, but we kept our mouths shut."

He took that without flinching. Yes, the error had been on his side, he said. He had been influenced by others in the family to speak against us. It was hard to believe our ears. There had never been a day like this. So much was changing, ourselves and Dad included.

❧ FOURTEEN ❧

How many children can really see their parents, or parents their children? One's eyes are always turned toward yesterday in this, not today, and most especially not tomorrow. None of us can clearly comprehend how the passage of the years affects everyone. Perhaps we refuse to recognize the possibility of change because change itself is not always welcome. If we are happy, we want happiness to last forever. If we are miserable, we often fear that any change will only be for the worse, so we prefer to endure a known misery.

Was it possible that Dad was beginning to see himself more objectively, his nature softening a little? A little, certainly, but not entirely. We were still a long way from each other. We were a family divided by circumstances which had lasted too long to be transformed in a day or possibly even in a decade. To Gerry, he remained aloof, seldom speaking, addressing him as *monsieur* if he did speak, leaving M. Allard to read alone hour after hour in the living room. Cécile and Yvonne, already overdue at the hospital, left the day after our meeting in the library.

Dad made one more statement to the newspapers. There had been, he said, "a misunderstanding." We posed with him for the inevitable pictures, which were taken to emphasize his point. Smiles were not evident on any face. Gerry held the photographer's floodlights. He and Annette stayed on for New Year's. There was no celebration to mark the old year or the new. The atmosphere within the Big House grew no warmer. In front of Gerry, Dad continued to speak icily about the eternal "outsiders" who could not restrain themselves from interfering with our lives.

The early months of the year saw Annette again in Nicolet, no nearer a personal solution of what to make of herself than before. Cécile and Yvonne were not far away from graduation. Marie, who pioneered many roads for us, knew that she must keep busy and make herself useful. For a Quintuplet to show any independence struck some of those around us as surprising. For Marie to launch out on her own they regarded as unthinkable. What she decided to do was to go into business for herself and earn her own living. She wanted to open a flower shop and work in it as the proprietor. From the very beginning, she ran into obstacles, some natural and arising from lack of any business experience, some deliberately created.

It was not such a wild idea as might have been suspected. Flowers had been an important element in our lives. We had been giving and receiving them at almost every public appearance. At home, a bouquet of roses for Mom was part of every important day on the calendar. We were well acquainted, as customers, with the florists' trade. But, to put her dreams into effect, Marie needed money, working capital, several thousand dollars of it, and here she immediately bumped up against the first obstacle, though there was something to the order of

$200,000 invested in her name under the terms of the trust agreements.

In those days, the trusts were supervised by the same standing committee, made up of Dad; his lawyer, Richard Donnelly; and a representative of the Guaranty Trust Company. Marie, blithely optimistic, believed that if she broached the matter tactfully she would have no trouble in being granted enough in the way of funds to launch the business. There were hours and hours of discussion devoted to the scheme whenever we were together in the apartment on Côte St.-Luc. Phil was drawn into it, and so was a girl we had met at Nicolet. Both of them were to work in the wonderful new shop, along with Marie. Nobody doubted that from the word go, all that was necessary was the will to succeed. Phil quit his job at the Canadian Broadcasting Corporation to go into training for his new career.

It would be best to begin the campaign for laying hold of the working capital by winning the support of Mom and Dad. Marie was hoping for their joint blessing and a vote in favor from Dad when she put the proposal up to the trust committee and asked for the release of a comparatively small amount of her inheritance. She took the train to North Bay, and Phil went along for company. She carried orchids as a gift for Mom and flowers for Em's grave. The conductor on the train apparently drew his own conclusions about the young man and young woman who rode along together, clutching bouquets. He smiled approval on them.

Phil's role, in fact, was that of escort only. He had to remain strictly anonymous and incognito. Mom and Dad had been told nothing about him, and this was certainly not the occasion to stir up fresh antagonism to any "outsider" or questions about boy friends. He was going to linger for an hour or so in North Bay, while Marie took a cab out to the Big House. At five o'clock, he was to engage another taxi and drive slowly past the gates. If she felt she needed more time to convince Mom and Dad, she would somehow signal him to go away and come back later. Marie picked up a cab from the station when they got off the train, and Phil wandered around town, up Ferguson Street and along Main, past the Empire Hotel on McIntyre and the *Nugget* office on Worthington.

At the prearranged hour, he rode out to Corbeil, peering anxiously out the cab window for some sign of her. She was standing with Mom and Dad on the driveway, just outside the garage. For a moment, Phil had no idea what to do, whether to have the driver stop at the gate or wait around the bend or what. Then Marie spotted him and, without a word or a second glance in his direction, quickly raised the door of the garage. Phil interpreted that—correctly, as it turned out—to mean that Dad would be driving her back to North Bay station. Phil had his cab driver hurry on ahead of them, and he hung around the station out of sight, until Dad's Cadillac had turned up with Marie.

She had had no luck at all at the Big House. Worse than that, some harsh words had been spoken about the venture she had set her heart on. Mom accepted the gift of orchids at first, then in the course of argument threw them out contemptuously. Nor would she hear of Marie's putting flowers on Em's grave. "People here would laugh at you," she said. "It would be much better if you gave your flowers to the Recluses for the chapel." So that is what Marie did. (The monastery set up in the old nursery had not yet been closed.)

At the station, Dad took a quick look at Phil, who was doing his best to appear inconspicuous, but to all appearances he was only a stranger waiting for the next train. Marie did not so much as turn her eyes in his direction. She said a quick goodbye to Dad, then she and Phil boarded the train separately. To maintain the pretense, they sat apart, though in the same coach.

It happened that the conductor was the same man who had smiled his benediction on them on the way up. He obviously fancied there had been a lovers' quarrel, and he shook his head sadly to see them. Only when the train had pulled out did Phil join Marie, to the romantic conductor's obvious delight.

When Marie applied to the trust committee for funds for the flower shop, she was turned down flat. They apparently imagined that this would be the end of it, but they had not recognized that their opposition would only strengthen her determination.

"Whatever happens, I intend to go ahead," she said. "I will not be stopped now." She proceeded to make her plans as though nothing had happened and the money was ready and waiting for her whenever she snapped her fingers. If she was refused the use of funds by the committee, there were other means of obtaining working capital.

But before anything else was done, she had to teach herself something about the sheer mechanics of running a flower shop. Gerry had a cousin who had a florist business in Sorel, which stands on the south bank of the St. Lawrence up toward Quebec City, as well as a brother who lived close by. For two months, with Gerry's help in advance, she stayed at the brother's home and studied at the cousin's shop. How to buy flowers at the wholesale market. How to keep them fresh and display them to best advantage. How to make up bouquets and table settings, wreaths and corsages. Phil, who knew as little about the ins and outs of the trade as she did, spent a week or two as a student in Sorel, too.

Gerry's cousin came down to Montreal, at the end of the seminar, to help choose the spot where the shop was to open. They found what they were looking for on the ground-floor corner of a new brick building in the St. Urbain district, close to four big hospitals, which would produce the right kind of traffic past the door. One could scarcely have discovered a more promising location. Marie signed a lease, and in the window of the vacant store there soon appeared a big hand-lettered sign: "Watch for the opening about May 10." That was Mother's Day that year, when business should begin with a flourish.

The name for the shop was part and parcel of the whole enterprise. It had been chosen at the very beginning, when the idea was beginning to germinate in Marie's mind. There was only one possible name for it: Salon Emilie.

Now the job of raising the money had to be tackled as a matter of emergency, with the deadline set for the opening. We each had a few hundred dollars to call our own on deposit in a North Bay bank. That was a beginning. We were delighted to contribute; in the outcome, Marie repaid every penny of it.

At this time, Dad had an allowance of three hundred dollars a month from the four of us, besides receiving five hundred dollars a month for the care of the property in Corbeil. This had been provided for at our request by the Guaranty Trust Company after Mom complained that it was hard for the two of them to make ends meet. We held a council of four to discuss what else could be contributed to the cause. The unanimous conclusion was that the three hundred dollars a month should be diverted for the time being to the Salon Emilie.

Inquisitive reporters were intrigued by the sign in the window. They knew where to turn for an interview. "Yes," Dad told them, "I am aware that Marie is opening a flower shop, but it is her venture, and anything about it should come from her." Marie was saying nothing yet.

She was a long way from having enough cash in hand to pay for the hundred and one items of equipment she needed. But, like the rest of us, she possessed a charge account at Eaton's department store, which billed the trust committee every month. That was a wide-open invitation, so far as she could see; credit was every bit as useful as cash in times like these.

With Phil's willing assistance, she shopped Eaton's from top floor to basement. They were in and out of the store, which covers a square block fronting on St. Catherine Street in Montreal. From the stationery department, she ordered note paper and billheads engraved with the salon's name and address. From furniture, she bought chairs and tables. She wanted counters, fittings, showcases; and she charged every single item on the list.

Annette went into the store one day with Marie, to look around the furniture department for some new chairs. The salesgirl recognized the two of them, as someone usually did when we traveled two or more together. The girl jumped to conclusions. "Which one is getting married?" she wanted to know. They smiled briefly, shook their heads, and departed.

The charge plate was punched a dozen times a day. All the bills, thousands of dollars' worth, were destined to be forwarded, in a normal way, to the trust company. They were due for a shock at the end of the month, but none of us felt Marie was wrong in the least. Whose money was she spending, anyway?

She liked to employ the same taxi driver for all her shopping expeditions. She left a standing instruction for him to collect her early each morning, because there was so much to do, and the opening date was drawing near. She had him wait outside every store or commercial sup-

211

ply house that she visited, and most evenings she worked through until close to nine o'clock. That meant sometimes that his meter had been clicking for twelve hours, uninterruptedly. It was not surprising that one month's taxi fares for Marie ran well over four hundred dollars. She had arranged for the driver to send her a bill. She forwarded it, of course, to the Guaranty Trust for payment.

It was a wonderful adventure. The other three of us had every bit as much fun as she did. For us, who had respected authority perhaps more than most people, Marie's defiant assertion of the right to do as she pleased was exhilarating. Her accounts of each day's excursions were listened to intently, often in peals of laughter. We could picture the faces of the trustees when the bills came home to roost.

As the deadline for opening approached, Marie moved out of the apartment into quarters over the flower shop. She plunged ahead and bought one more vital piece of equipment for the business: a brand-new Chevrolet station wagon. That came on credit, too—a little money down and a long time to pay. It might have looked more impressive to have a name painted on its side, but the only fitting one would have been "Eaton's."

The trouble was that none of us could drive. We had never been given lessons, and up to now we had lacked the nerve to try. Gerry could handle a car—his father had run a wartime trucking business in Drummondville—but as a student he lacked a license. Phil had no license, either, and could not drive, but before long, from necessity, he became the self-taught chauffeur, picking up flowers from the wholesale markets, on credit, of course, and making deliveries to customers.

With one other girl assistant, who had had experience working in florists' shops, they opened the Salon Emilie on Mother's Day. They had spent much of the previous night putting in the last-minute touches to have everything ready. The newspapers covered the event as if it were the dedication of a new town hall. Everyone who came through the door was handed a big red rose as a souvenir. Some people were spotted coming back time and time again, collecting a bouquet flower by flower, but Marie was too thrilled to complain. The first day's business showed a deficit of six hundred free roses.

Mom and Dad sent not a word of good wishes for the success of the flower shop.

Annette, away in Nicolet, rounded up a big order from the graduating class at the Institut Familial. The corsages and flower arrangements they wanted were worth two hundred dollars. But the order came in only a few hours beforehand, so all other business at the shop had to be suspended while every hand turned to making up the flowers. Nicolet was a long way off, down Route 9, which has a dark reputation as a dangerously fast highway, where cars speed along at seventy miles an hour and more and accidents are frequent.

"But we have to go, anyway," Marie told Phil as they worked frantically with wire and scissors, gardenias and camellias. Phil and a driver's license were still strangers to each other, but they loaded the station wagon with the orders, then added more flowers as a present from the Salon Emilie. They raced out of Montreal, over the great arch of the Jacques Cartier Bridge that crosses the St. Lawrence, out on the road to Nicolet, with Phil's foot nudging down the accelerator pedal. The wagon raced up to the entrance of the college with only minutes to spare. Annette, waiting anxiously there, doubted that Phil could ever stop without smashing into the wall. But stop he did, with a squeal of tires, and he and Marie scrambled out to deliver the consignment.

213

Annette rode with them back to Montreal, always happy at the chance to break the monotony of life at the Institut. Phil's luck held until another car edged out of a side road. There was an alarming sound of metal scraping metal. It was impossible to tell whose fault it was, but Phil could see his immediate future in terms of the nearest police station. Their hearts accelerated even more rapidly than the station wagon, until the two drivers agreed that no real damage had been done and there was no need for anyone to linger until a patrol car passed by.

But for the wonderful, slightly scarred wagon, Annette would have spent the twenty-second birthday alone in Nicolet. After the flower shop closed for the day, Phil and Marie got busy. There were flowers to make up, balloons to inflate, a cake and a bottle of champagne to buy. Then Cécile and Yvonne joined the party, and off we went through the night down Route 9 again. Boarders and nuns were fast asleep when the wagon reached Nicolet. The town's many clocks were striking midnight. A telephone call made in advance by Phil ensured that the domestic-science room, which was the place most closely resembling an apartment, would be left unlocked. We crept upstairs with all the trimmings, set out flowers on the tables, hung up the streamers and balloons. Then one of us tiptoed through the halls to surprise Annette. She came into the now transformed room with a delighted smile breaking on her face. So as not to wake the whole college, we could only whisper, "Happy birthday!"

Our lately acquired knowledge of how other people enjoyed themselves was spreading, like ripples on a pool after a stone is tossed into the water. The compulsive need for privacy was slow to change, however, and we nursed our secrets. The newspapers continued to interest themselves in any detail, true or fanciful, of our existence that they could scratch up. One reporter who stormed the apartment caught a glimpse of a pair of shoes on the hall floor and mistook them for ballet slippers. The next morning, we were greatly intrigued to read that the Quintuplets had realized a childhood dream and were busy taking dancing lessons with eyes on a stage career.

Among Phil's friends there were several newspapermen who would have been delighted to reveal the story of the girl with whom he spent most of his evenings. At Cécile's urging, he worked at the shop under a *nom de plume*, or perhaps *nom de fleurs* is a more accurate description. "Tremblay" is a name that fills column after column of the Montreal telephone directory, as common in French Canada as Brown or Jones would be elsewhere. Philippe Tremblay was Phil's chosen pseudonym, to make it difficult for anyone to find out there was romance mingled with the scent of flowers.

Dad had made a habit of turning up unannounced and unheralded in Montreal to check up on what we were doing. We were not always ready to see him. Two of us once hid in our beds in the Côte St.-Luc apartment, scarcely breathing, while he pounded on the front door and then went off in search of the superintendent and the pass key. But the superintendent was our friend. He would let nobody in without first asking us if we were agreeable to seeing them.

When Dad stopped by to inspect the Salon Emilie, Marie was out shopping—where else but at Eaton's?—and a girl assistant was in the shop alone. Somehow, on the trip to Montreal Dad had heard whispers about Phil and Cécile. It would be wrong to single out anyone for blame, but after Dad left the shop and the city, it became clear that somebody who knew a great deal about us was reporting to him regularly by telephone.

215

We suddenly felt that we had lost our cherished privacy, and we had good reason to. It slowly dawned on Phil that he was being watched. Whenever he moved about the city, he was under surreptitious inspection. A series of men were spying on him, looking exactly as they do on television, in trench coats and hats with brims turned down. Beyond the shadow of a doubt, this was at Dad's instruction, because the private detectives were charged to us. The bill for their services was included in the annual statement of accounts that was submitted to each of us under the terms of the trust agreements.

In the course of her training, Cécile had been transferred for a while from the Hôpital Notre Dame de l'Espérance to another hospital for extra experience. At her new address, the St. Jean de Dieu, she was called one night to the telephone. It was Dad calling from the Big House, and his voice was chilling.

"I know everything about you and that man in the flower shop," he said. "I know he is really Philippe Langlois and you are his girl friend."

Only Dad could have passed this on as a tip to the newspapers immediately following the call. The telephone at St. Jean de Dieu rang again for Cécile. This time it was Phyllis Griffiths, long distance from Toronto.

"Is it true," she wanted to know, "that you and someone named Philippe Langlois are going to get married?" The question was premature. Nothing had been settled. It was possible, by stretching the truth a little, to say "No," but a complete answer would have been "No, not yet."

The only possible thing for Phil was to go and confront Dad, to introduce himself for the sake of Cécile. She took him first to meet Pauline, who was then in the Convent of Bon Pasteur, in Montreal. Pauline telephoned the Big House and announced that Philippe

216

Tremblay-Langlois was going to make the journey north by train, alone. He left in such a hurry that he forgot to make a note of Dad's telephone number, which was not listed in the directory. He had to call Cécile from the station when he reached North Bay, before he could let Dad know that he would like to see him within the next hour or so.

Phil could make no pretense of being brave. When he got out of his taxi at the gates, he was trembling like a leaf, pale of face and moist of palms. The watchdog lurking behind the fence looked as threatening as a man-eating tiger. Half running up the driveway, Phil was certain that he was being watched from behind the curtains of the front windows.

Mom opened the door and with no further ceremony led him straight to the library; it turned out to be the only room in the place that he saw on this visit. Dad was waiting there for him, and his greeting was grim-faced. Mom watched their encounter. So did Victor and Claude. To Phil, it seemed uncomfortably like the start of an investigation by the Spanish Inquisition.

"I hear that you are aware that I am Cécile's boy friend," he said, nervously. He waited for some response, but there was none. Dad seldom was in any hurry to speak at times like these. "Well," Phil continued, giving up the hope that anyone would help him out, "I should like to say that Cécile asked me not to work at the flower shop under my true name. She was anxious to avoid publicity. It was done for the best of reasons, because she wanted to embarrass nobody . . ."

They heard him out. The only questions Dad had to ask were about the running of the flower shop. He was polite enough and not openly hostile, but Phil felt chilled to the bones. Forty-five minutes or so later, after a formal goodbye all round, he was back in a taxi, return-

217

ing to North Bay station. The formalities had been observed and he had at least met the parents of the girl he would marry, even if he appeared to have made no great impression on them.

The summer came, and Annette once again found time, weeks and weeks of it, hanging heavy on her hands. Marie was being kept busy fourteen and fifteen hours a day at the shop. Cécile and Yvonne were fully occupied. Only Annette, with classes over at Nicolet, had virtually nothing to do. She was bent on one thing, and that was to stay away from Corbeil, which represented the past, from which she had not yet completely extricated herself. But she would need a reason for staying away. Otherwise there would be fresh arguments with the family. She wanted to keep the peace with Dad and Mom, and she wanted, too, to see whether she was capable of earning some money, a few dollars, anything to bolster the sense of independence. She was still the untried one in this respect, unprepared for anything resembling a career.

At Joliette, on the shores of Lake Assumption, some fifty miles from Montreal, a camp for crippled children is open for two months every summer, for boys in July and for girls in August. It was operated as a charity for the inmates, but counselors there receive ten dollars a week. Annette, with many qualms, applied for a summer job, copying a leaf from Phil's book and calling herself Annette Lupien. To her joy, mixed with trepidation, she was accepted.

Miss Lupien, undetected by any reporter under her assumed name, spent a rewarding season at Joliette. She discovered one or two more strands in her personality. She could get and keep a job, if she had to. She could conquer her qualms about looking after children who were deprived of infinitely more than the Quintuplets ever had been, of the ability, for instance, to run on legs or touch with their hands. At the close of the summer, she told the rest of us a great deal about the camp. The following year, she was busy with a hundred and one preliminaries to getting married, so in her place Yvonne worked at the same camp on the shores of Lake Assumption.

In spite of all the effort and concern Marie put into it, the flower shop refused to prosper. Perhaps one explanation lay in the nature of flowers themselves and the response that the proprietor of Salon Emilie had toward them. The roses and carnations and peonies and the rest that Phil brought in by the armful every morning in the station wagon—he had a license now—made it seem selfish to have them only for sale. Some of this beauty surely should be spared for friends or for the altars of churches in the city. Sometimes a nun who came through the door needed money for a good cause, and that could usually be spared somehow from the cash register.

It did not take a genius at arithmetic to tot up the figures and find that income did not match outgo, that there were few days when enough money was taken in to pay the bills. But it was not yet time to call it quits. In the trust fund, there was more than enough to guarantee that every creditor could be paid. So, when one wholesaler cut off credit because his bills were overdue, another could be approached. The list of suppliers had by no means been exhausted yet. Dropping one source and picking up another simply meant that Phil had to change his morning route when he went out for the flowers.

But that next winter brought chills that were more than the flower shop could withstand. Marie once more approached the trust company for money to be released to her. She met the same unsympathetic response as before. Now there was not enough coming in for the payments to be met on the station wagon. When the inevitable happened and it was repossessed, she resorted to hiring taxicabs to drive to the markets for fresh flowers and to make deliveries to loyal customers. The taxi fares often amounted to more than the price of the bouquets.

Yet, one wholesale house was impressed by the potential of the Salon Emilie to the point of offering to finance it and manage it if only Marie would stay on there. A letter saying this much was sent to the trust company. A successful business could be built up, it indicated, provided someone with more commercial experience could turn a hand to it. But Marie had no desire to continue on those terms. A few days before Christmas, it was clear that the only alternative was to close the doors for good. The day after Christmas, the Guaranty Trust issued the formal announcement that the experiment was over, but there were struggles ahead in squeezing out the money to make sure that no creditor suffered.

The death of the flower shop was a bitter blow to Marie. To this day, she does not like to dwell on the subject. Yet in the light of after events, it can be seen only as a victory, scarcely as a defeat. In the opinion of three of us, it marked Marie's final break with the frustrations and fears of being a Quintuplet. The experiment was worth far, far more than it cost, for who can set a cash price on freedom?

At first, she tried to find herself a job as an employee in another flower shop. At Mimosa Fleuriste, on Rue St. Denis, she worked briefly, under an assumed name to shield herself from the probing questions of strangers. Whether or not Dad pierced the disguise and found out who "Denise Mousseau" really was, we did not ask. But detectives were put on her track, and the bill turned up on the annual statement as before.

She had lost weight noticeably over the past months, and she was too frail to continue working for long. We think she neglects herself and eats too little when she is left alone. For more than a year after leaving her job, her time was spent between sharing another apartment with Annette and Cécile, and spells confined in the hospital.

⋙ FIFTEEN ⋘

Another Christmas came and brought with it another attempt to keep the peace between ourselves and the family. The four of us spent December 25 together in Montreal, then a few days later Annette and Marie took Gerry to Corbeil. At this second meeting, the two men, Gerry and Dad, both strong-willed and both used to expressing their feelings forcibly if the need arose, collided head on shortly after they set eyes on each other.

"At least he will know now what kind of wood I burn in my fireplace," Gerry told himself as some sort of consolation.

First there came the family blessing, an old French custom for this season of the year which we Dionnes faithfully observed. The children gather in the living room and kneel before their father, asking his benevolence for the year to come. As a member of our generation and a close friend, Gerry went down on his knees beside us in front of Dad, who raised his hands over our bowed heads as tradition demands and said, "May God bless you and assist you in all you do throughout this New Year."

The words had scarcely been spoken before the first signs of stress appeared. Mom was whispering none too softly to Annette, "I did not think you would be foolish enough to come back with that one." From then on, Gerry could do nothing to please. He tried to make friends with some of our young nephews and nieces who had come up to the Big House with their parents for the holidays, and he suggested that they call him *mon oncle*. The family thought that was presumptuous in the extreme. He tried to make a joke or two with the wife of one brother, and that was frowned upon as though he were the villain of an old-fashioned melodrama complete with black mustache.

To break the ice and start up a conversation, he launched into his favorite theme, as well as the subject of his college courses, philosophy. He landed knee-deep in trouble again. He was only showing off, they said, with his long words and fancy talk, and besides his so-called scientific opinions were plain nonsense. Annette, who had held out some small hope that he would make a good impression, could not hold back her tears.

Dad saw clearly enough that Gerry's intentions were serious, and he did not hide his reactions. "You are only interested in Annette," he said bluntly, "because of her fame as one of my daughters and because of her money."

He may have realized that this was perhaps the last time he would have the opportunity to do battle over one of us. He had fought so skillfully and successfully in the past, defeating all who opposed him. Now he had lost us, as he interpreted it, to the ceaseless plotting of "outsiders" like this talkative young upstart from Montreal, and he was jealous and angry. His anger took him one step farther. He would not permit his house to be used by Gerry for his courting, he declared. He knew

223

there was a romance going on between them. It was sinful, and the priest would be told about it. He shouted these accusations, and Gerry shouted back at him, outraged that his sincerity and motives should be doubted.

"If I wanted to abuse your daughter, Mr. Dionne, I had a million chances in Montreal. Do you think I would be crazy enough to do so under your own roof?"

Now Oliva joined in. He stands at least as tall as Gerry, a hefty six-footer, and he was seething with rage. "Look, my friend," he said, "that is enough. If you come here to argue, why not go back right now to Montreal? And I will help you on your way."

Mom managed to restore the peace for the time being, but it could be no more than a temporary truce. That same night, Oliva drove the two visitors to the station. It was useless to pretend that Gerry had won any favor in Dad's eyes, though he could scarcely make sense of the antagonism. As usual, the family put on the masks for the benefit of the world. The newspapers could smell marriage in the air, though Annette herself was not so sure. After the storm, one of the family was questioned by a reporter about the outlook for a wedding. The bland reply was that the romance between Annette and Gerry was "an eminently desirable attachment to which no objection could be taken."

A Catholic with problems to solve is encouraged to make a temporary retreat from the demands of the world and, in a convent, find the quiet she needs to search her soul. Annette made her retreat in Nicolet. She had to satisfy herself that Gerry, with his forceful and forthright attitude toward life, was the right man for her. Should she marry him? Could he make her happy? More than that, should she marry at all? Was that a path to happiness and peace within herself?

Marriage in our faith means children, and there was a subject fraught with fear. We had always accepted without question the forecasts made in our babyhood and repeated on many a subsequent occasion that the Quintuplets could never bear babies. A French biologist, an acknowledged expert in his studies, put it more brutally than anyone else. Twenty-three years earlier he had said, "They will certainly never be able to lead normal lives, much less able to give birth." Those were indelible words. If we had been able to achieve a certain normality at this point, would it be trying good fortune too far to look toward marriage? What kind of marriage would it be if there were no children to bless it?

In Nicolet, Annette found no more encouragement. The Institut Familial had been greatly changed and modernized in the rebuilding of the town after the disaster, but the advice the nuns there had to give her carried a fundamental flavor. "Forget Gerry," they told her, "and throw yourself into the arms of God." It was not easy to come to a decision. Sometimes it seemed to her that choosing Gerry was the worst kind of foolishness, even something close to blasphemy. But, inevitably perhaps, she chose marriage with him. There are many ways to think of God and to have trust in His charity.

That autumn Annette and Gerry were engaged. Before they were married, she had much to tell him about the old, unforgettable years in Corbeil. They spent a great deal of time with Father Lalande, who listened with endless patience to her story. His counsel had not changed with the passage of time. "Do your best to maintain good relations with your family. They are your parents, and nothing alters that fact. Whatever your feelings, you must forgive if you would be forgiven."

There was another theme to which he returned repeatedly: "If your father had been a clever man, a rich man, a real money-chasing businessman, he might have shown no mercy and exhibited you for his profit. He might even have allowed you to be shown as freaks in a circus side show, to the degradation of you all. But he was only a simple man, whom life changed, as it changes all of us."

We used to spend hours in speculating what might have happened if Dad had known no need of money at the start, like the father of those other quintuplets, the two brothers and three sisters Diligenti, who live in Argentina. The Diligentis sent a cablegram when Em died, but we have heard nothing of them directly. Their father sent the children to separate boarding schools under disguised names, so that their relationship was not known to many. They saw each other only on holidays.

In one of the scrapbooks we have, there is a quotation from an interview he once gave. "I had to make sure," he said, "that they grew up as independent personalities, free from a quintuplet complex. Now that they are men and women, they must learn to fly on their own wings." Without knowing him better, it is impossible to tell how or where he learned such wisdom.

Annette left the Institut for the last time that June. The urging of Father Lalande weighed heavily on her and Gerry. "Maintain good relations . . . Forgive." After Gerry had finished his course at the University of Montreal—he had transferred there from St. Laurent—they made another trip to see Dad. Gerry was working now at the Beneficial Finance Company in Montreal, and he had bought a new car. They dared not risk aggravating Dad's suspicions by arriving unchaperoned, so they drove to Corbeil with a friend of Annette's and one of Gerry's brothers. If there was not safety in numbers, at least there was some reassurance.

The news they brought for the family was that they were going to be married, and in one week's time. The reception they received was about what they had anticipated. Why marry Gerry? Why must they marry so soon? Why had they kept their intention a secret until now?

Annette did what she could to explain. She had given much thought to the idea for months past. Gerry was now in a position to support a family. They had not wanted to announce anything because, if possible, they would like an inconspicuous ceremony, without publicity or reporters or an army of cameramen. Dad seemed to approve of that.

Yet, as a family, we had a habit of making things complicated for each other. Before Annette and Gerry had reached Montreal on their return journey, Dad had told the story of their forthcoming marriage to the newspapers. More than that, they had gathered the impression that he would not himself be at the church. So once again, the typewriters started clicking and tongues began to wag.

Gerry was living with a brother, waiting to move into an apartment of his own. The next morning, he was called to the telephone. "Is it true," a reporter demanded, "that you are going to marry Annette Dionne?"

The future bridegroom imagined that the family would keep the secret until after the ceremony. He thought that the reporter was simply fishing for information. "There must be some mistake," Gerry said. "I believe I would be the first to know."

So the newspapermen went back on the telephone to Dad, who only reaffirmed what he had said the day before. Now it was Gerry's turn to be badgered again. They must have scented another, typical Dionne confusion in the making. Gerry could only confess the truth. The only shred of a secret remaining was where the ceremony would be held. He clung to that, planning to invite, under pressure, only one television crew, only one reporter apiece to represent the major Canadian and United States news agencies.

Annette, who was living with Marie, had chosen their own parish church, Notre Dame de la Salette. It was only two years old at this time, a modernistic building with bright mosaics stretching across its front, standing on Park Avenue, not far from St. Catherine Street. The altar is placed in the middle of a circular sanctuary, and there is a reception room in the basement.

She explained to the church authorities that she wanted as quiet a wedding as would now be possible. They thought that the best thing to do would be to lock the front doors, to discourage all but family and the handful of invited guests. Annette felt hopeful that the simple ceremony she had wanted might still be possible. It was an empty hope.

There were more complications than anyone might have suspected. Three days before the ceremony, Yvonne was hurried by ambulance into the Hôpital Notre Dame de l'Espérance as a patient, dangerously ill with pneumonia, which had developed after an attack of Asian flu. Mom and Dad finally agreed to come down to Montreal for the wedding, but for the time being they were withholding any enthusiasm for the event; not until much later did Mom let Annette see the happiness she felt for her. And, of course, the newspapers traced where the wedding was to be held without the need of a formal announcement.

By nine o'clock of the morning of the wedding, a shirt-sleeved television crew was inside the church setting up lights and equipment. Minutes later, the advance guard of reporters turned up. When the main doors were closed as arranged, later arrivals with notebooks and pencils simply slipped in through the rear entrance.

Meantime, a crowd was gathering outside the locked doors, peering through the little glass panels set in the woodwork. There was muttering against the Dionnes. "Why have they locked the doors? They are people like anybody else. We should be entitled to enter whenever we please. If we can't go into this church when we want to, we should go elsewhere." Fortunately for her already shaky composure, Annette heard nothing of this, nor of the rumor that had spread in the city that it was Cécile who would be the bride.

Among the sightseers pressing against the doors was a member of the congregation named Florian Houle, an inspector on the staff of the Quebec government. Marie had not yet met him, but within a year he would marry her.

At the altar stood Father Lalande, in the congregation sat Dad, with a rose in his lapel, and Mom, wearing a corsage of the same flowers. The television lights glared and the flash bulbs popped and Annette became Mrs. Allard, with joy in her heart but permitting none to show in her face. She wanted to run outside and try somehow to talk to the crowd, explaining this happiness that she was what any girl would want to be, a married woman, not just one among five but one among millions and millions. But Dad was watching, and he would not have approved of an outburst like that.

So, after the reception held in the basement room with a crowd of newspapermen as uninvited onlookers, the bride and groom slipped away. They went straight to the hospital with Mom, Dad, Cécile and Marie. A "No visitors" sign hung on the door of Yvonne's room. She had been put in an oxygen tent. The nurses let Annette and Gerry in to see her for no more than five minutes. There was no telling at that point what turn she might take.

The honeymoon was a strange mixture of pleasure and fear. Fear demanded that the radio in Gerry's car should play constantly so that no news bulletin would be missed. They dreaded hearing, as a kind of price for their happiness with each other, that Yvonne was dying. They had to be ready to turn back to Montreal at any minute.

Gerry's brothers needed to be driven home to Drummondville, so the honeymoon began there, in a motel. Annette discovered that Cécile had been having a fine time with the luggage, sewing her new nightgown into knots, hiding among the clothing the usual lighthearted surprises designed to bring a blush to the cheek of any bride.

In the morning, Gerry stopped at a cigar store to buy a copy of each of the Montreal newspapers, which had spread the story and pictures of the wedding over their pages. The clerk behind the counter was thumbing his way through one of the versions. "This fellow who married the Quint comes from Drummondville," he said conversationally, not recognizing Gerry. "He must be a lucky guy to get himself fixed up with a girl like that."

Elsewhere on their trip, which took them wandering through Quebec, they were recognized constantly. But the radio had brought no news of Yvonne, which meant that she was holding her own, and Annette found herself enjoying a little, for the first time, the sensation of being looked at by strangers. Their glances were so discreet and well-intentioned that nobody could object.

Setting up house, however, was something else. The apartment they had hoped to move into was not ready. For two long weeks, Gerry continued to room with a brother, while Annette stayed with Marie. Mr. and Mrs. Allard met each weekend in a Montreal motel.

A few weeks later, the headlines blossomed again, proclaiming a SIMPLE, LAVISH $10,000 WEDDING FOR QUINT CÉCILE. The difference was that nobody was upset by the furor. Phil wanted to make something of a splash, and Cécile was anxious to please him. Possibly because he had not antagonized Dad by speaking out so loudly and clearly as Gerry, this marriage ran into far less opposition from the family. Cécile did not go near Corbeil until she had announced in a letter to Dad what she intended to do. She left no room for argument. His permission was not asked. "Why should I do that?" she said to us. "I am over twenty-one."

The wedding was to wait until she and Yvonne graduated as nurses after their three years of training. Mom and Dad did not come down to see the two of them receive their diplomas at the ceremony in the Church of Notre Dame, but they did send flowers. Gerry sat in plain view in the audience—this was the month before he married Annette—and so did Phil. Cardinal Leger, in gleaming red against the sea of nurses' white, made the presentations. Cécile and Yvonne had satisfactory marks in the 80's, Cécile with awards in psychology and hygiene, Yvonne receiving a Medical Council prize in orthopedics.

The future Mr. and Mrs. Langlois already had been given a useful start in furnishing their new home. They were the slightly astounded owners of some furniture from the Big House. It signaled a great turn in the lives of Mom and Dad. Mom often complained about the considerable cost of keeping up the place, as she had done before we were aware that the bills were met from the trust money. In all seriousness Mom used to say, "There is only one thing for it, and that is for us to move down into the basement. There is no other way to cut expenses—unless we can get more money somehow." Now, after fourteen years in a home no cozier than a hotel, they had admitted to themselves that the Big House was much too big, and it was pointless to stay on there.

The new house that Dad designed for himself was halfway up before we so much as heard about it. It was a gray brick bungalow, standing on a rise some five hundred yards from their old home, with a stand of pine, spruce and maple pressing on the back door. From their

231

windows they could overlook the mansion they were leaving, as well as the whole area where the farmhouse once stood, and the nursery and the souvenir stands. "We believe we shall be very comfortable," Dad said, "and we also believe we shall have more privacy." And perhaps as many memories as ever.

The question was what to do with twenty roomfuls of furniture after they had chosen what they wanted to take with them. We settled it all in writing, so that there could be no misunderstanding. On our behalf, would he please decide which of the family and which of us was to receive each unwanted piece? Dad liked that, as a token of respect for his judgment.

Not long before Annette's wedding, he shared out the pieces. Annette asked for her collection to be stored in the basement. Poor Mom could scarcely bear the thought of parting with some of it after all. They went down together to look over what was now Annette's. "Keep everything," she said. "I'm not really interested." Mom was not sorry to have it back.

There was a single exception. Each of us accepted gladly the crib she had slept in so long ago, each with its painted scroll praying, *Que le bon Jésus vous garde.* Mom kept Em's, which we accepted as right, too.

Phil was invited to New York to appear on a television show. He went along with our brother Victor and Camille Henri, of the New York Rangers ice-hockey team. The three of them were wanted for *To Tell the Truth*. Who was the real Philippe Langlois? The show's panel had to judge. Cécile was urged to go, too, was even offered a free honeymoon trip to tempt her, but the process of breaking out of our shells was incomplete. She said no to all public appearances, though the wedding would have to be included as a distinctly public event.

They went back to the Sacred Heart Church in Cor-

232

beil for the great day. The priest who conducted the ceremony was another link with old times: Father Paul Sylvestre, who, as a newly ordained curate, had taught us the catechism. Television cameras were there again to stare at every moment and spread the news to all Canada.

Cécile wore a dress of peau de soie covered with Swiss lace, studded front and back with hand-sewn pearls. Mom wore a black dress that was already in her wardrobe; she had been sent a dozen dresses to choose from by the salon in Montreal that made the trousseau, but she did not particularly care for any of them.

Yvonne was only just recovering from pneumonia, too weak to leave the city. Marie had no wish to attend. So Annette was the only one of us to see Cécile married. She came up with Gerry the day before, wearing for the first time a new fur coat she had bought months earlier. She was delighted with the results of her shopping, and so were the weighers of souls at the Guaranty Trust. When they were presented with the bill, they thought it was "very reasonable" and were pleased to tell her so.

Possibly it is the northern climate, the endless winters, the short-lived warmth of summers, that makes some hearts so cold in Corbeil. There is something in the air that inhibits rejoicing. It showed up clearly at Cécile's wedding. The Irish families in the neighborhood came around to smile and wish her luck. Most French Canadians turned their backs, as if they wanted to have no more to do with us. Some were not slow to complain to reporters, who paid the usual attentions, that they had not been invited as wedding guests. Some who were invited did not attend.

In the car on the way to the snow-covered church, Cécile waited for Dad to say some word of kindness, to wish her well, to give her his blessing. He sat as silent as ever, his feelings locked inside. When the reception, at

233

the Golden Dragon restaurant in North Bay, was over, Cécile deserted the crowd. In the lonely cemetery in Corbeil, she laid her bouquet on Em's grave, which was bare of any other flowers.

In the forlorn, never-abandoned hope that some shred of privacy might be within reach, nobody was told where the honeymoon was to be spent. None of us had ever learned that it was useless to try to throw off the pursuit. At the first motel Cécile and Phil checked into, the room next door was taken almost immediately by newspapermen, so Mr. and Mrs. Langlois drove through a pelting rainstorm for sixty-five miles to find another spot to stay.

The speculation was that they would make for California. In fact, they went for one night to Niagara Falls, a convenient break in their journey apart from all other considerations, and then on to New York City. They arrived at three o'clock in the morning. Six hours later, tracing them by some wizardry, two local reporters hammered on the door of their hotel room, demanding an interview.

Phil, rubbing sleep from his eyes, spoke to them through the door. "Come back at twelve and you shall have our decision." This was a net the two of them were determined to escape. They threw their clothes into their bags. Phil telephoned down to the desk for his car to be ready for leaving within minutes. The hotel clerk wasted not a second in spreading the news. When Cécile and Phil emerged from the elevator into the lobby, a host of the press was waiting for them.

With the help of Arthur Sasse, a photographer from the New York *Daily News*, whom we had known from Corbeil days, they moved to a more discreet hotel, fending off the inquisitors as best they could. From their new sanctuary, they risked emerging to see some of the sights of the city. One of those sights was the show at Radio City Music Hall. Waiting on line, they heard two elderly

234

women who stood just ahead of them talking to each other.

"Did you know there's a Quint in New York?" one asked the other.

"Maybe she'll come here to the Music Hall," said the other.

Florida was the destination Cécile and Phil were heading for. On the way down, in a restaurant not far from Washington, a waitress restored the faith of the bride in the fundamental kindness of ordinary people. The girl served them their meal without a second glance in Cécile's direction. But over coffee, she put a slip of paper into Phil's hand. On it was written a single word: "Congratulations!"

After Florida, they drove north again, more than two thousand miles to Corbeil. The Big House stood empty behind its fence, a shell where footsteps echoed on bare boards and windows were locked tight against the penetrating frost. Most of the furniture had been moved out, but the bedroom of Mom and Dad had not yet been completely emptied.

The new bungalow had only three bedrooms, and with Claude and Victor still living at home, there was no room to spare. The only place for Cécile and Phil to spend the night was in the old house, in the bedroom of Mom and Dad. Before they turned in that night, they explored the place from top to bottom, peering into every room from attic to basement, with Cécile dropping a word or two about this event or that which had taken place between these walls.

It was one way to begin exorcising memories.

◄§ SIXTEEN §►

Cécile and Annette had an ambition in common. They set out to become the most suburban of housewives, indistinguishable from young brides anywhere. Mr. and Mrs. Langlois lived in a house which they helped to decorate themselves, like any newlyweds in an advertisement for paint or wallpaper. The Allards lived in the long-awaited apartment, where Annette had to resist the temptation to telephone her husband in the middle of every morning at his office.

Cécile braved the hazards of beauty parlors, where sitting under a dryer sometimes seemed like sitting in a ducking stool waiting to be dumped into the water of unwelcome attention; as a precaution, she was likely to make the appointment for a certain "Mrs. Tremblay." Annette gave up her music lessons, put her domestic-science lessons into practice, and listened to the soothing strains of FM radio. And of course, we stayed close to each other, all four of us, not physically so close as before, but not a millimeter farther away in our thinking.

It surely is not unusual for a young man and wife to

explore each other's minds as part of the fascinating process of discovering each other. It is not always easy, but it is always good to learn how to trust another person. With Phil and Gerry, Cécile and Annette relived the past, memory by memory, unraveling the skein. The nursery, the Big House, the ignorance, guilt, fears—they were spoken of with hesitation in the beginning, then more freely as the habit of sharing confidences grew. There cannot have been a more loquacious start to many other marriages. Even Gerry, who we consider can out-talk almost anyone when he tries, was sometimes out-classed as a conversationalist.

Of course, there were some small, sweet secrets that we held to ourselves. One was that Marie had met Florian Houle at Mass at Notre Dame de la Salette. They had been to the movies together. They had even mentioned marriage, Marie confided to us, "but you are not to say a word about it, not to anybody."

She passed along that secret a matter of two weeks before the day chosen for their wedding, but this was nothing for a new husband's ears until seven more days had passed.

For once, of all marvels, nothing went amiss with a Quintuplet's desire to enjoy a modicum of dignity and have some respite from sensationalism. Marie made her preparations carefully with Florian. They would become man and wife in the secluded Sacred Heart Chapel of the ancient Church of Notre Dame, the great, gray Gothic pile facing the Place d'Armes, in the old section of Montreal, which looks far more French than Canadian. Only after the event would the newspapers be told about it, in a formal, brief announcement.

The evening before the ceremony, she delivered into Gerry's keeping the typewritten statement and a photograph, to be released to the Canadian Press. A handful of friends were given the date, in the middle of August, but as extra insurance against word leaking out too soon and the risk of another publicity circus, they moved forward the day by forty-eight hours.

Two days before that, Marie wrote to Dad. Until then, he had no clue to her plan or to the existence of a suitor in her life. She was fearful that again he might attempt to influence her future, so her letter was deliberately timed to arrive after she became Mrs. Houle.

None of us went to the church. Much as the wish was there, the only chance of giving Marie the anonymity she had set her heart on was for us to stay away, because the sight of two or more of us together was sure to attract attention. When the parish priest, Father Jean Baptiste Vinet, pronounced them man and wife, two altar boys served as the witnesses.

They drove off for a ten-day honeymoon, congratulating each other on the smooth working of their plans. They had covered many miles on the road toward Lake St. John before the car radio began to proclaim that now a third Quintuplet had journeyed to the altar. Yet the frustrated reporters were not entirely deprived of grist for their mills. Dad had a remark or two to make for publication: "Mrs. Dionne and I have not met the young man, and we did not know that the marriage was going to take place. If Marie picked him out by herself, we feel sure she will be happy."

Not long afterward, they did meet Florian. His job took him away from home one week in every two, driving for hundreds of miles on inspection trips through the province. Most of the time, Marie went with him. Being at home with only the telephone to talk to was a dismally lonely business when he was away. On one of his trips, they came within striking distance of Corbeil. This was just the opportunity, though Marie could scarcely bring herself to accept it, to go and meet Dad. She knew too well how Gerry had fared, and he had not married a

Quintuplet without preliminary examination by the family. Florian might be treated even more brusquely.

They drove slowly past the bungalow, Marie hoping without admitting it that nobody would be home. But Dad's latest Cadillac was parked in the driveway, and so was Victor's Ford Meteor. And when they took a second look, there was Dad, up on the roof, fixing a television antenna.

"It would be better to turn back," Marie said.

"When we have driven so far, that would not make sense," said Florian.

To Marie's pleasant surprise, it was by no means a disagreeable meeting. Dad seemed to find Florian not unlikable and even invited him to stay and talk longer than time allowed. Not until later did Dad, who likes to find what he considers to be apt descriptions of people, decide that Florian "looked like the devil in holy water."

The time soon came when the three of us who were married had to face the prospect of bearing children. What was impressed most deeply on our minds was the pessimistic forecast made by scientists long before. Much more recently, at the Hôpital Notre Dame de l'Espérance, a nurse had said just the same thing—that Quintuplets could not become mothers. The thought had done little to add to the contentment of being married.

With that in the background of one's thinking, one's heart can find only diluted joy in pregnancy. Cécile and Annette were both fearful, Cécile no less than Annette, in spite of her hospital training. Only Marie, whose turn came later, was unafraid at the prospect of childbirth.

If we thought about the choice instead of about the apparently inevitable disaster, we each would have liked our first-born to be a girl. The reason was simple enough: she would be christened Emilie. The dream was one of

239

the fancies, idle and otherwise, that a woman cherishes to brighten the nine, nervous months of waiting for the unknown. But much stronger, more possessive thoughts haunted Cécile and Annette.

Cécile had no doubt that she would die in childbirth, which she was going to experience first, according to the calendar. She clung to the hope that she might be permitted to live long enough to see the baby she was to bear, but she felt she could count on only perhaps a moment or a minute or two at best. In case time was as short as that, she had to be conscious to the very end. If she had to rouse herself from anesthesia, assuming that were possible, she would lose precious seconds.

The answer was natural childbirth. She felt she had no choice. Every week she went for instruction in how to govern her breathing, how to relax mind and therefore muscles. She made an odd discovery. The company of other women, going through the same routines as she, did something to ease her anxiety and build up her frail hopes.

On September 15, 1958, with Phil by her side massaging the muscles of her back, she was taken to St. Justine's Hospital, where she and Yvonne had spent part of their training. The two sisters were together again in the delivery room, Cécile the patient, Yvonne scrubbed up and wearing surgical mask and gown. Though she was not a theater nurse, Yvonne had asked for this privilege to attend Cécile. It had been willingly granted.

It was a long and not an easy labor. Yet the hope that had been planted in the past few months grew stronger hour by hour. When it was over, and a seven-pound-four-ounce boy lay in his mother's arms, Yvonne shook with sobs of exhaustion and joy which she could not control.

Cécile was calmer than she. "How marvelous it is to watch the birth," she said wearily.

Later, Annette and Gerry came in to join the new parents in toasting their son in champagne. On the bedside table stood a bouquet from Phil that had been waiting for Cécile in the room when she was wheeled back from the theater. With the flowers was a card that said *Merci*.

The fears of Annette took a different turn. She had seen Cécile disprove the old tales of death and sterility. Annette felt certain that her child would be born alive, but deformed. The early months were difficult, and the conviction about being delivered of a crippled baby dwelt in her mind.

All of us are unduly sensitive to pain, cowards perhaps, as a result of the years spent in the atmosphere of a hospital, among nurses and doctors who discussed and charted the least indisposition. It shows in peculiar ways, this antiseptic upbringing. Annette, for instance, has the impulsion to brush her teeth after every meal and between times, too. If she does not, she feels a sense of unease. And possibly the careful washing of hands several times a day is the mark of a Quintuplet.

To help calm her thoughts, Gerry took her driving in the evenings and on weekends, long drives along the highways to nowhere in particular, letting the hum of the tires and the movement of the car smooth away anxiety. As late as the eighth month, the obstetrician said there was no harm in it.

In the course of the ninth month, Gerry hurried her to the Sacred Heart Hospital in Cartierville, as expected. They sat together in the labor room, holding hands. "Now breathe deeply," he kept reciting masterfully, matching his breathing to hers. On November 2, 1958, Jean-François Allard was born, as lusty then as he has been all along.

Yvonne came to the hospital, in the hope of watching over the second sister as she had watched over the first. She arrived with her uniform over her arm to help in the delivery. The doctor was content to let her in, but the

241

authorities said no. She was not on the staff there, they explained, and therefore it was not possible. It was a great disappointment. It would have been a climax to nursing for her and a temporary farewell to the profession. After her illness at the time of Annette's wedding, she was not physically strong enough to take up her career again.

Dad saw Jean-François when he came down with Mom some months later and put up at a motel. "Take the baby in your arms," Mom urged him. He took his grandson from her and inspected him carefully before expressing an opinion. "Well, he seems to be clever," he finally concluded.

Now there were two boys in the next generation of us, but not yet a girl. That was left to Marie. She lost her first baby in a miscarriage, but that did not dismay or deter her. A second pregnancy ended the same way, but her determination was unaltered. On Christmas Eve, 1960, the most wonderful day of all time for her, a daughter was born to Marie.

She grew up bright and gay as a bird, darting around the house from the moment of waking until she was put protestingly to bed. She slept in the crib that was once her mother's, with its blessing, *Que le bon Jésus vous garde.* Is there any question about her name? It is, of course, Emilie.

There are probably as many kinds of love as there are people who come to experience its powers. To each of us, it dawns brand new, as if it had been invented uniquely for oneself. Three of us have known what love of and for children of one's own means to the peace and fulfillment of life. There is nothing more important to us than this today.

Yvonne's life has been different. When she found that nursing was a closed door to her, she had to direct her mind in other directions. For a while, she studied wood

242

carving as a pupil of Jean-Julien Bourgeault at the colony that his father, André, founded at St. Jean Port Joli, on the bank of the St. Lawrence, down toward Gaspé. Sculpture from that workshop is sold all over Canada. Each of us has a carving done by Yvonne, an animal, a bird, a human figure, and visitors admire them. But making such things was not the answer for her, any more than her painting had been.

With a friend she had met while nursing at St. Justine's, she went off in a car—Ivy is the only one of us who can drive—to see some of the sights of North America. She drove as the fancy took her, and eventually they reached Florida, whose promise of sunshine holds a permanent fascination for northerners like us. They stayed on there for a while, soaking in the sun, fishing, sailing, until the desire came to head north again, to familiar places.

Yvonne made the decision that Marie and Em had reached before her. With her friend, she entered the Convent of the Little Franciscan Sisters at Baie St. Paul, which stands on the river downstream from Quebec City, almost opposite St. Jean Port Joli. As Sister Marie Thierry, she hoped to be able to nurse handicapped children. She wrote to Dad, "I have thought about it a lot, and I prayed, and I believe I have been called." Those were almost the words Marie had used once before.

Living in the convent was as arduous for Yvonne as for Marie. She had thought that her training as a nurse might be useful. There turned out to be no opportunity for employing it. Loneliness was a problem of its own, as it is for each of us when we are too long apart. Whenever they could, Annette and Gerry went to visit her. When they arrived during one weekend, Yvonne broke the news that they had almost anticipated. No matter how much she would have liked to stay, the nuns wanted her to leave them. "It is not the place for you," they said.

With one small bag to carry and the rest of her luggage to follow, she left the convent alone, hiding her disappointment in silence, as Dionnes do. Annette and Gerry took her home with them to the brick-and-stone bungalow they had bought in St. Bruno, ten miles from the Jacques Cartier Bridge as it leaves Montreal. The plan was to set up a workshop for wood carving in the basement for her, close to the spot where Gerry stores one of his particular treasures, a birchbark canoe in which he goes hunting when autumn comes.

But Yvonne could not find contentment there. Suburban life did not attract her. She seemed to be poised between the material world of babies and laundry and marketing and a world within herself. Five months later, she went back into the Church. From a nun she had known in Nicolet, she heard of the Convent of the Sacred Heart near Moncton, New Brunswick, seven hundred miles away. A new hospital was to be built there, and Yvonne might be able to work in it.

Annette went with her to the train to say goodbye. For Annette she left a souvenir, the earthenware bowl from which, in Baie St. Paul, she had eaten every meal.

⋖§ SEVENTEEN §⋗

During the writing of this story, a double event occurred to set the world thinking once again about
the mysteries of quintuplets. In the course of a single
week, the 57,289,761-to-1 chance that used to hold such a
fascination for Dad came off twice; the odds against that
must be incalculable. On September 7, 1963, the five
Prieto boys were born in Venezuela. Seven days later,
the Fischers—four girls and a boy—arrived in Aberdeen,
South Dakota. Suddenly it seemed that there was getting to be a crowd of the likes of us!

Every baby is a marvel of survival and a joy whether
born in a hospital, a palace, or in a cattle shed. When the
miracle of birth is multiplied, a certain bond links the
families. They face a test of the spirit, the parents now
and the children later, which only this handful of people
are ever allowed to experience.

Because we are of their generation now, we can imagine to some extent the pride and anxiety that Mr. and
Mrs. Andrew Fischer must have lived through and will

continue to live through, in all probability, for the rest of their lives. The Fischers, the Prietos, and the Dionnes encountered the same, rare challenge.

We wondered, not too seriously, whether it might be arranged for us to meet, family with family. But we have not met, and it is much better this way. If there is anything helpful to be said, it is more easily done at a distance than near at hand, though we would hope to speak as friends, not strangers. Perhaps it is not too great a conceit to hope that as the Fischer Quintuplets grow up, they will avoid some of the mistakes that we Dionnes made.

The mayor of Aberdeen was kind enough to invite us to visit there. The town had just named itself "Quintland." That was the name engraved on his invitations and it stirred so many memories. Thirty years ago, "Quintland" was Corbeil. We were invited down to join in the party and parade on "Fischer Quints Day." But three of us in Quebec and Montreal could not leave our children, and Yvonne could not undertake such a journey from the convent near Moncton, where she works in sight of New Brunswick's rolling hills and wide skies, where the pattern of the seasons, sighted from a plane, looks like a tapestry of God.

We all knew it was best to stay away from Aberdeen on that occasion. That was a day for the happy new generation of quintuplets, not for us. But both the Prietos and the Fischers were in our thoughts. We celebrated for them in our hearts.

The parade and the party must have been a wonderful, fitting way for a town to celebrate and wish five babies health and happiness. Everyone believes that the birth of quintuplets is something to commemorate for its rarity. The difficulty is that nobody really knows how to raise them as human beings, rather than as money-

246

making curiosities. There is no chapter by Dr. Spock or Dr. Gesell for bewildered parents of quintuplets to turn to. What few books exist on the subject of multiple births are ponderous medical tomes with little to say about safeguarding the spirit of the children themselves. And even the best-stocked medical library contains no more than a slim volume or pamphlet or two about quintuplets. In modesty, it may be said that the only reliable books concerning them are medical studies of the Dionnes as babies and small children.

It is to be hoped that the doctors and nurses watching over the Fischers and the Prietos find some interest in all the charts and statistics the Dionnes' physicians compiled, but it is doubtful whether the parents will discover much consolation there. Possibly, however, there is something to be learned from our own lives and what happened to our family, the errors that were unwittingly made, the things done, and left undone.

There were parallels in the circumstances of the families. Like us, the Fischers come from rugged, peasant stock. All three families knew poverty, though the Prietos, existing in a mud hut in a slum of Maracaibo, tasted it most bitterly. Andrew Fischer struggled to support a big family on take-home pay of $76 a week. That much money would have seemed like a fortune to Dad when he was earning four dollars a day hauling gravel in the years before we were born.

The Dionnes and the Fischers are all children of the woods and farms. They had cows and chickens and dogs waiting for them when they went home from the hospital. Dad used to take us out looking for deer tracks in the fields. Jean-François, Annette's eldest, already likes to struggle to lift up his father's empty rifle. Claude, who is Cécile's first-born, plays soldier, with a flourish of salutes. Marie's two daughters are gentler souls.

247

It would be overwhelming to visit the new Quintland, which by all accounts is not so unlike the old. The greatest difference probably is in medical facilities. X-rays gave Mrs. Fischer warning that she was carrying five babies, and her husband said she cried all night. Mom had no such notice in advance, or she might well have wept, too, and longer. There were air-conditioned "isolettes" in readiness for the Fischers and incubators for the Prietos, which are improvements over butcher baskets set by a kitchen stove.

Quintland, South Dakota, developed much as Corbeil did, a busy, mushrooming place where everything takes on a lopsided look, as though seen in a mirror maze at a carnival. Quintuplets clearly have the ability to bring out the best and the worst in people. Charity flourishes along with greed. Good-neighborliness matches gross self-seeking. Real friendships grow side by side with the exploits of men seeking to get rich in a hurry at someone else's expense. And—who knows?—in Quintland the hearts of men may sometimes be changed and the dross in human nature transmuted into gold.

It was good to read that the blessed spirit of charity flourished, bringing a cascade of gifts from friends, neighbors, and well-wishers all over North America. We heard about the pledges of money, materials, and workmen's time given to building the Fischers a new house, about the Venezuelan government paying the Prietos' medical bills and setting up an educational trust fund, about savings accounts by the dozen being opened, baby food by the case, toys, medicine, furniture—and free haircuts for the Fischers for years to come.

If our experience is any guide, not all motives in Quintland are so charitable. There is the risk that the flavor of sawdust and circuses will gradually dominate the original, spontaneous celebrating. Quintlands are

248

magnets for lawyers and promoters and men who wave checkbooks and try to take a profit from human lives. When a family is poor, five extra babies can create a desperate need for money to be found somewhere. It is a terribly dangerous situation. Quintuplets can so readily be turned into a bonanza for all kinds of people. The dividing line is thin between meeting real financial need and cashing in on an opportunity.

In the case of the Fischers, and also apparently with the Prietos, something existed from the start which was not there in Corbeil. This was the belief that the babies would survive. Nobody thought there was a chance for us at first, so perhaps there were bigger temptations in 1934.

We have learned that a price must be paid for everything. This is as true in Aberdeen as in Corbeil. The highways they build into Quintlands to bring in the tourists are paid for by the children and their parents, who are caught in the glare of public curiosity. The chamber-of-commerce spirit keeps them in the spotlight, whether they find it agreeable or not, when the factories pour out Quintuplet dolls and souvenirs and the curio shops open up to sell them.

In due course, the Fischers and probably the Prietos will discover for themselves the overwhelming power of public curiosity. It is not possible to imagine its strength unless one has felt it personally. It is the force that conjures up the contracts that put the pictures in newspapers and magazines and on television screens. It sends advertising agencies hurrying to obtain endorsements for a hundred different nursery products. It is mighty enough, unless the parents or guardians are very watchful, so to contort lives that quintuplets are not thought of as people but as a tourist attraction.

Public curiosity is a tidal wave that will threaten to

swamp the new quintuplets sooner or later. They can only learn how to float on its surface until they grow old enough and strong enough to swim against the current, if that should be their wish later on in life.

The decisions their parents take in the first few years will probably be the most important of their lives. It is so difficult, but so necessary, for them to think in terms of the children's lifetime, not only of the immediate, urgent future—whether this contract should be signed or rejected; whether arrangements might be made for the babies to be put on display or allowed the privacy of normal childhood; whether they will be brought up together with their brothers and sisters or apart; whether they will be protected from the world or whether the fear of kidnaping or some other harm may be measured against the sense of timidity that springs up like a weed in children who are too closely guarded and supervised.

If we could stand by the cribs of the new generation of quintuplets, like fairy godmothers in an old nursery tale, what wishes might we have for them? The first would be for them to grow up as independent beings, linked by great affection to their families but each able to stand sturdily alone. This would be a very special wish, because if anyone made such for us, it has not yet come completely true, not after all the years that have passed.

We would wish that there might be money enough to shield them and their families from want or temptation, but not so much that anyone forgot that money is never a substitute for human warmth, tenderness and understanding.

Faith would certainly be our wish for them, so that whatever the future holds, there will be dignity and meaning in it.

Another wave of the magic wands would make sure that they are regarded as people, not characters in a living legend, as we once were. Quintuplets are all too often thought of as animated dolls who remain babies forever. Or, worse still, they are considered to be something apart from the race of mankind, suffering none of the pains and problems that everyone else must share. In the first hours after we were born, we became a legend. Nobody did anything to prevent more legends accumulating until they threatened to stifle us and everyone around us, including Mom and Dad.

Telling the truth then becomes a hazardous task indeed. In the fall of 1963, when part of this story was told in a United States magazine and the newspapers seized on it, the myth of the Dionnes exploded like a bomb. To judge by the headlines, it was as though we had set out to prove that Little Red Riding Hood was a witch in disguise and Santa Claus the wolf who gobbled her up.

We have no wish, no desire, no intention to hurt anyone, particularly not Mom and Dad. What is said in these pages has to be said for the sake of a generation not yet old enough to read far beyond ABC, the children of Annette, Cécile, and Marie. It is unthinkable for them to grow up in a world of deliberate falsehood. May the new quintuplets be spared this necessity of destroying legends. But if the need arises to recognize and spell out the truth, perhaps it will be remembered that it is a process like undergoing certain medical treatments, painful at first but healthy in the long run.

On the day last year when the headlines about us were blackest, a friend came to visit us and talk until two-thirty in the morning about what occurs when a myth is exploded. Another, who had often heard our confidences in the past, wrote us a letter from Ottawa. Each of them said the same thing: "What has happened now is for the best."

The world must not be deceived, they said, into be-

251

lieving that there are special, fortunate beings, spared every pang of mind and body, who dwell in some kind of earthly paradise. No matter if you are pauper, President, or Quintuplet, you can live only in terms of faith and hope and charity. You must build your life—and this is no easy thing for anyone—on the rock of truth, not on quicksands of pretense and deceit.

Possibly, if all goes well, the new generation of quintuplets will turn out to be what some people dreamed we might become, citizens of the world, ambassadors of good will between nations. That would be our wish for them, too, if they were so inclined.

And there is one other, which is expressed in a song often sung in Quebec. In French its title is "*Que reste-t-il de nos amours,* which is familiar in English as "I wish you love."

Looking back now is like remembering strangers. Sometimes late at night on a television show, there are the old movies of five little girls in identical clothes with identical smiles and identical curls. It seems that they could not possibly be us but some rare, legendary children from an age of innocence, saved for always from growing up.

The properties in Corbeil are the last financial ties with long ago. Dad no longer sits on the trust committees which still supervise the Quintuplet money. As his influence fades, he mellows. The lean, piercing look is vanishing little by little as his face fills out and age adds weight to his frame. Sometimes there are hints that he thinks he might perhaps have made mistakes, but he is not one to admit such things.

Mom has changed less than he. She is as devout as ever, at a loss to understand our generation, eager to talk about the good old days, as she remembers them, before all the trouble began. She knits beautiful shawls and baby sweaters for her grandchildren, and she loves to put on a pair of old slippers to rest her feet when she comes on a rare visit to one or the other of us.

If Dad were prepared to listen, what might be said to him about the mistakes that everyone made? That we were all caught up in a situation which nobody could fully understand. He did not anticipate how much the world would be interested in his five unexpected daughters. He tried to keep us in seclusion and, in doing so, thrust us away from him. Because we were taught always to hide or scurry away, publicity relentlessly pursued us as dogs will chase a running child.

By no choice of his making, Dad was compelled to fight so hard to win us back into his keeping as a kind of prize that he locked us up too tightly and, when people tried to interfere, denounced them as "outsiders." He was reluctant to give us up even for marriage. He wanted us for himself as long as he lived. He did not see the good things that were associated with our birth. If he has been unhappy, this is one of the important reasons. We did not ask to come into the world.

Poor Dad. He could have had such a beautiful life.

The money that poured in was both a good thing and a bad. Good because it took the edge off the poverty our family lived in and made material living comfortable for everybody, ourselves most of all. But it was bad because it changed Dad's nature. There was so much more money than love in our existence. It took a long time to realize the effect it had on all of us and an even longer time to begin to feel the stirrings of compassion, to believe, as the French Canadians say, that perhaps we should "put a little water into our wine."

It was a mistake, clearly, to treat five individuals as though they were only five parts of a single being, and virtually everyone concerned with our upbringing fell into this error. Today, the differences between us are more obvious than before. Physically we are not wholly identical, no matter what the nursery doctors concluded.

We certainly look like sisters, but we take different shoe sizes, vote for different political candidates at election time, think somewhat differently, except on some occasions.

There does come the odd moment when one can sense what another is thinking without a word being spoken and across considerable distances. If the telephone rings in Cécile's house in a Quebec City suburb, she often knows it is Annette calling. The two of them, unknown to each other, once bought identical blouses, one in Quebec and one in Montreal. One Christmas, all four of us brought home the same kind of white table radio as a surprise for each other. Can this mean that some degree of telepathy operates between us? Who can accurately say? But in moments of stress, we can sense most strongly, miles apart, what one of the others is experiencing. Sorrow perhaps travels farther than joy.

In some things, after marriage, we are closer than before. In the loyalty between us. In our reluctance to hurt each other with a thoughtless word of cruelty, or to let any argument between us last very long. In our need for each other's affection expressed in the simplest, smallest ways, like a telephone call, a letter, a greeting card bought on an impulse and put into the mail.

Three of us have been blessed with children. Little Emilie has a sister, Monique, into whose crib she sometimes scrambles at night. Jean-François has two brothers, Charlie, with the unmistakable eyes of Marie as a child, and Eric, born in September, 1962. Claude Langlois has his brothers Patrice and Bertrand; there was a twin to Bertrand, but he died at fifteen months old. They have a baby sister too, Elizabeth, who is a beauty and is called Babeth.

It used to seem that all the three of us needed to do was live in the present, letting each day bring its measure of work in the house, shopping, caring for the children, looking after a husband, seeking ourselves as individual personalities. This was precious happiness, of course, and because faith means a great deal to us, more now than before, since it is founded on experience of life, we said our thanks in our hearts.

Yet the world does not stop turning. One's life continues, and each of us hopes to go on growing toward maturity. The future was once a frightening thing to contemplate. Not so, however, these days. Now if those close to us can be patient and we can hold on to what has been granted us, tomorrow is something to be dared, not to be daunted by.

Not long ago, a young Massachusetts housewife wrote a letter to us, recalling the days of her Depression childhood when "work was scarce, food was low, winters were cold, and money was practically nonexistent." But her mother spared five cents for a book of paper dolls called "The Dionne Babies." "For me," the young housewife wrote, "the Quints were five fairy princesses, dressed in lovely clothes, that I could only dream about, and I went through every phase of growing up with them . . . The money, which messed up your lives for you, also was your ticket to freedom . . . Without all the hated publicity, people like me would have been deprived much pleasure."

She concluded, "I'm sure you feel fortunate now, to be so special, because even though you lost your individual identities, you acquired an identity that belongs to you alone—the Quints. No one will ever be quite that special again."

So, perhaps the legend served a purpose in its day, if it

255

brought a touch of sunshine to someone. Perhaps now the truth, as we have seen it, will serve a deeper purpose too. In some ways we *are* special people. So is everyone else on earth, unique in the eyes of God.

Who can say that her search for herself is ever really ended?